CW00548176

ENLIGH

AS HELL

HOW TO BE
SPIRITUAL

AND NOT BE A
D*CK

DR. TONY ORTEGA

By The Author School

Published by Ink!

2022 Text @ Dr. Tony Ortega
2022 Cover Design @ Helen Braid 2022

A CIP catalogue for this book is available from the British Library.

Typeset in Garamond Classic 11.25/14 by Hewer Text UK Ltd, Edinburgh

Paperback ISBN: 9781399930161

By The Author School

ink! By The Author School
Kent, England, United Kingdom
Email: inkpublishingservices@gmail.com
Website: www.inkpublishingservices.co.uk
Twitter: @services_ink

In Loving Memory Of
Sonia Ortega
3/4/1965 – 4/30/2022
Daughter, Sister, Mother, Grandmother, Cousin and Aunt

In the short period of time since you left, your presence has
been missed immensely. Rest in Power sis.

"That through the radiance which was once so bright be now
forever taken from my sight. Though nothing can bring back
the hour of splendor in grass, glory in the flower. We will grieve
not, rather find strength in what remains behind."

William Wordsworth

INTRODUCTION

For most of my life, I tried to uncover the secret to what spirituality meant for me. I was raised in a fairly strict Catholic household. The God I learned about during this era was one who hated gay people, and every time you thought about premarital sex, you had sinned. Well, sh*t, I was sinning at least 152 times a day. Tell this guy not to do something and I just want to do more of it. How could I believe in this God? How could I practice something in my day-to-day life that was all about kneeling, standing, and sitting, while waiting to commit cannibalism?

Moving to a more Christian-based faith in my early adulthood, I still got the 'God doesn't like the gays' speech but it was less intense and therefore less scary to participate in. Yet, the speaking in tongues, and attendees falling to the ground after the pastor prayed over them, left me wondering: is this faith or schizophrenia? It all seemed so out there.

Later, when actively participating in a twelve-step fellowship and working my second step, I was told I could create the God of my understanding. This appealed to me on so many levels and I went ahead and created a Higher Power based on Superman. Around this time, I was introduced to Buddhism as well. The problem was that despite the fact it all resonated with me so much, I still had the instilled Catholic guilt that would not allow me to really embrace these new philosophies and make them my new normal. Yet, with my twelve-step work and my rudimentary knowledge of Buddhism, I started to get a sense of what I really connected to and a small taste of how things could look on street level.

Circa 2004, hot off the heels of one of the worst breakups of my life and a major relapse into drugs and alcohol, I came across Marianne Williamson. She kept speaking about a text she studied called *A Course in Miracles*. I decided to pick that up and quickly put it down, as it was way too dense for my barely sober mind to grasp. Plus, the *Course* kept using the word Christ and this just triggered my Catholic PTSD. Marianne stayed in my head, though, for many years. She planted a small seed in me. More on that in a bit.

What followed were many years of sheer avoidance of all things spiritual due to personal traumas and a four-year descent into the deepest depression I have ever experienced in my entire life. I was able to come out of that with the help of a guy I was flirting with to make another guy I was having sex with jealous. The one I wasn't sleeping with caught on to my game and decided to be a friend. I am forever grateful for his altruism. He asked me to start juicing (green juice, not steroids) and meditating. Now, if you know anything about Cubans, we never eat anything green and we can't stay quiet for very long. Fortunately, I had the gift of desperation and decided to give it a shot. I tried one of Oprah Winfrey's and Deepak Chopra's meditation challenges and found it to be fun. Deepak has a very soothing voice and I kind of needed that. Plus, he seemed really down to earth. I didn't feel like I needed to spend seven years in Tibet to get the concept of meditation. Green juice, not so much, but boy, did I shed those 30 pounds I'd gained in four years.

My meditating friend had gone to a book signing one evening and he posted a picture of him and the author—Marianne Williamson. Yes, her again. She was launching her new book, *The Law of Divine Compensation*. She just couldn't leave me alone. I felt like she was stalking me. I decided to buy the new book and immediately fell in love with what I read. I started to devour all her books—most importantly, *A Return to Love*. This particular book is what she calls the *Cliff Notes* for *A Course in Miracles*. I made the decision after reading *Return* to actually pick up the *Course*. It took nine months to read, but it almost felt like a modern-day version of the Bible. Yes, the use of the word Christ continued to trigger me to all hell. Yet, all the religious things I had been taught throughout my life were brought to the present and in a much more relatable way. And best of all, there was nothing about gays burning in hell.

I later met another *Course* teacher, Gabby Bernstein, and devoured her reading material. Her stuff was a bit hard to internalize as it felt like it was written for straight, cisgender, heterosexual women. However, she also came from a twelve-step background and was a New Yorker. I participated in her master classes and joined the community her fans had formed. This was very cool, as I was reintroduced to crystals and introduced to energy healing, tarot cards, oracle cards, angels, and mala beads (Buddhist prayer beads). It was like; as long as the practices involved preaching love, nothing was off the table. They were huge fans of Kundalini yoga, which was a bit of a turnoff for me. For whatever reason, I shy away from trendy stuff. What I enjoyed the most was being free to express my spirituality however I felt was right for me, with no punishment from God.

I went on to do many training programs in different disciplines. I wanted to learn it all and see what was right for me. I studied Reiki and reading tarot, oracle, and angel cards. I even got crafty and started making bracelets and malas. I felt great. I also started to see deeper meaning in the most mundane things. However, because of my spiritual beliefs, I sometimes struggled with how to make it look less lofty and less out there. How could I relate to my fellow gay men and still do everything I loved? The main struggle was how to make *this* my own.

The most disheartening thing I then saw was how fake the spiritual and personal development community became. They were mostly all di*ks. People with a weekend of training started to sell courses that were not only way too expensive for common folk, but weren't at all evidence-based. These individuals would shame potential clients by saying things like, "If you are not willing to invest in yourself and your transformation, then you need to look at why you care so little about yourself. You could find the money." One spiritual leader would tell attendees in their live seminars to use the technology they just learned (again, over the course of a weekend) to coach others. As a licensed mental health professional with a doctorate degree and almost three decades of actual mental health experience, I dropped my cup full of celery juice (the Flavor Aid of the spiritual community) and said screw this. I didn't want to be associated with fakes. They were just a bunch of di*ks looking for money and social media likes.

Then came my breakup of 2016 and my family estate war of 2017, and the split from my spiritual community occurred. I started to dislike everything even remotely associated with my former community, even though so many of these practices were around long before they were. But I didn't care about that. I needed to find my own way. Then—BAM, the world experienced the global pandemic of the coronavirus. It gave me some pause to reflect on my life and how I wanted it to look. It made me miss all the things I used to love and now rejected for silly reasons. It was time to get hood and make my own manual that brings not only spirituality but psychology to a very street level. Here are ways spirituality can look in your real world and not just in a yoga studio, temple, or over-priced weekend course. Ready to get Enlightened as Hell?

CHAPTER ONE

Identity: Who Am I? No, Really, Who the F*ck Am I?

"Impersonating Beyoncé is not your destiny, child." - RuPaul

Any fan of *RuPaul's Drag Race* will tell you their favorite episode of the season is likely the Snatch Game episode. This is the episode in which the queens are challenged to impersonate a celebrity and make Ru and the guest judges laugh their collective asses off. As many queens will tell you (I'm looking at you, Kenya Michaels) they are not always successful at being someone else. This is analogous to real life in many ways. We can never truly be successful being someone else (except queens like Adore Delano). We are all so busy trying to be someone based on societal or familial standards, as well as what we think is expected of us on social media, that we have no answer to the question, 'Who am I? No, really, who the f*ck am I?'

Whether we come from a background of trauma or not (and the definition of the word trauma is quite personal and broad), we have to recognize that we have a very human side to us. This comes with a genetic predisposition for fear (discussed in Chapter Three). Most life forms have the ability to feel fear. As small children, we internalize and absorb so much scary information that it accumulates into the foundation of who we are. The information we receive can be seemingly innocent and meant for our own good, yet when it goes through the filter of our young minds, it can become distorted.

5

Fears, traumas, wounds, and any other negative experiences start to join and eventually take on a form in our 'basement'. It has become a big, dark monster and it is now a permanent resident of our psyche's home. This resident likes to remind us of past negative events in our lives, to prove to us we are not good enough. We start to believe the inner negative chatter and believe others know it all about us as well. Our identity is compromised by the negative chatter and self-misperceptions. This resident becomes your inner victimizer.

> #ElevateNOW: The monster we think we are
> is not who we are. This is not your identity
> unless you choose to make it such.

Once we understand this about ourselves, we need to build support structures to quiet the roar of the inner victimizer in our basement to a dull murmur. We may never be able to get rid of it permanently, but we can get it to STFU.

You may know the inner victimizer by other names. Freud called it the unconscious. Jung referred to it as the shadow. The Jedis referred to it as the dark side. RuPaul regularly uses the term inner saboteur. For the purposes of our journey here, we will refer to it as the inner victimizer.

The first step in getting very clear on our identity is knowing we have everything we need. We just need to access it. We saw this about ourselves and others during the coronavirus pandemic. Folks were forced to up-level their game to deal with living in quarantine conditions with some degree of success. We have what it takes; we need to dig deep and grab it.

It seems we are always searching for something. This could take the form of needing to know the why of something. This could also be when we seek other people to fill something within us that we perceive we are missing and/or lacking. It becomes a journey of seeking less of what we need and more of whom we need to be. We have the blueprint to our own lives. We don't need someone and/or something else to tell us otherwise. If we go within and allow ourselves, give ourselves permission, we can uncover any answers in time.

The inner victimizer does not allow us the freedom to create that person we want to be. It reminds us of all the times we have failed. But we haven't failed—we have figured out ways in which things haven't worked. We can't make it look just like so-and-so did it, yet this does not mean it can't happen. Let's keep the goal and modify it so it is ours and it looks our own way. Then we won't perceive we are lacking something. If we just take a moment to quiet our minds and separate ourselves from the inner victimizer, the right answers will emerge. Listen to the softer voice, always.

#ElevateNOW: Remember, our fears will speak in a very loud voice. Our true identity speaks in a softer, lower voice.

Additionally, let's look at all the wonderful things you have accomplished in your life. None of us can be great at everything. Yet, we are great at some things. Even if just one thing—it's the thing *you* are great at. Stop focusing on your weaknesses and double down on your strengths, even if it's just one. So, when the inner victimizer wants to tell you that you don't have what it takes, remember your strength (even just the one) and say to the inner victimizer, "Thanks for sharing, but I am doing this (insert strength you want to double down on) instead."

The next step in developing our identity, is to remember: "No one is better than me and I am better than no one." We are all equals. Yes, you read that right: we are all equals. Sure, we may look different, yet how we operate as human beings is all the same at a cellular level. We just don't think so because the inner victimizer walks around with a measuring device to gauge us against everyone else. We are so used to carrying around our own ruler all the time. We suffer from a chronic illness and its name is comparison. We never seem to stand in our own power and recognize our greatness.

> #ElevateNOW: When we are feeling bad about ourselves, we need to stop and see where we may be comparing ourselves to someone else. Then, drop the measuring device.

These behaviors are always based on comparison. We are our own worst enemy, judge, and critic (the three main personalities of the inner victimizer). We think others have it better than us, or that others have more luck than us, or they have more power or ability to do and/or be something, and we have none of these. If we were more able to sit in our own power and just look at ourselves, and just ourselves, we would be able to know who we truly are. This is the time to break the measuring devices we use against others and instead see our magnificence.

This levels the playing field and reduces the tendency to compare and despair. There is a saying that goes, 'Comparison is the thief of joy'. Of course, you are not going to feel happy when your measuring device is out against the world. How can you fulfill the first step (I have everything I need; I just need to access it) if you think you are less than (or even better than) other people? Take an honest appraisal of what you have and look at it with objectivity instead of with the blinders that the inner victimizer has set up. If we are pounding ourselves down incessantly while comparing ourselves to others, we are using those blinders.

Now, we could also go in the other direction and think we are the hot sh*t and act like buttholes around others. Let's get a grip here. When you elevate yourself at the expense of someone else, it is no better than doing the reverse. If we see what we have in common with our fellows instead of our differences, the tendency to feel like a piece of sh*t around others decreases exponentially.

> #ElevateNOW: When we allow ourselves the ability to look at ourselves through a more objective lens, what can we see? Someone who is beautiful, amazing, and unique.

Does it look different than someone else's identity? Sure. Does that diminish yours? In no way, my children! There could be so many circumstances behind another person's success and identity that you may not be aware of. We don't know anyone else's full story, so let's not do ourselves an egregious injustice by engaging in any comparison. If we get very clear on this, we won't make judgments about the movie of your identity based on someone else's movie trailer.

Now that you have made it this far, you can get to the next step, which is, 'I don't need to be cured or fixed'. There is nothing wrong with your essential self, which is your inner champion. This really speaks to a concept from *A Course in Miracles*, 'The Christ in me cannot be crucified'. The Christ reference translates in real-world terms as our essential self. The part of us that is whole and complete.

> #ElevateNOW: Our essential self is not broken. No one can touch that except ourselves. Our thoughts and behaviors are the things we need to work on.

We have collected a series of labels throughout our lives. Some of these labels were given to us on purpose, and some with malice. Some we internalized from life experiences and traumas. This only results in establishing a passive form of victim mentality in which we feel there is something wrong with us. There is nothing ever wrong with us as a person. While we may need to make some significant modifications in our thinking and our behavior, there is never anything intrinsically wrong with us. We are never broken. We are not our symptoms or behaviors.

A Course in Miracles also states our only problem is our belief in separation. This separation can be from a power greater than ourselves and/or even seeing ourselves as separate from others. This is one of the ways we continually see ourselves as separate and less than others—thinking we need to be fixed or cured. While from a medical perspective this may be the case, as many medical conditions do require treatment and a subsequent cure, this does not apply to our mental/emotional/spiritual bodies. Who we *are* is never broken. Who we *are* is never sick. Assigning this level of frailty to our essential selves, aka our inner champion, gives fuel to the inner victimizer.

> **#ElevateNOW: What needs to CHANGE
> is the way we think, see, feel, and do.**

There are simple steps we can take to decrease the power of this thought, yet it feels difficult because it is so different from what the inner victimizer tells us. While we often have no control over our initial or primary thoughts and feelings, we have full control over the secondary ones. For example, if you are cut off in traffic, your primary thought and feeling will be anger. This is out of our control. It is instinctual and part of that genetic programming. Don't judge yourself for this. We can feed our primary emotions

10

and even increase them through our thoughts and behaviors, such as cursing them out or trying to cut them off.

What needs to change here would be the secondary process. Even this does not require fixing or curing, just a simple tweak in a direction that allows us to feel more empowered by who we want to be and not by the situation at hand. In very simple terms, THERE IS NOTHING WRONG WITH US. What could be considered 'wrong' (and this is a tough word used currently as an objective adjective) is how we allow ourselves to think, feel, and do. This can always use a change—no fix or cure needed.

For those of you wondering how to better cope with traffic issues and be enlightened, you would need to just follow a few steps. The first is to breathe. When we have traffic-related tension, we are not breathing appropriately. Secondly, don't make it about you. The traffic jam was not caused on purpose to create anxiety, and the person who cut you off did not do so as a personal affront to you. They are selfish d*cks. Lastly, remind yourself who you are and who you want to be and make the next right choice that is in alignment with this.

Now, the last step in knowing our inner champion is the 'I don't NEED anything outside myself to make me feel better'. Sadly, we have become a society of externals. Whenever we feel bad, we seek something external to make us feel better and, at times, whole.

> #ElevateNOW: Being Enlightened as Hell
> means we sit with ourselves and work through
> whatever we are going through without reaching
> out to something external to feel better.

This is not to say we shouldn't use our support system. I encourage reaching out to good friends. However, we need to watch our reliance on them as well as our reliance on any number of other things. We can want external things to make us feel good but wanting and needing are two very distinct things. Wanting is desire, while needing is requirement.

> #ElevateNOW: The one thing we do NEED to do more often is to go within more than we do right now.

A more permanent solution would be to go back to the third step, to change the way we are thinking and doing rather than escape the feeling. While it would be nice to have that cocktail or that new blouse, these are just the condiments of life, not the meal.

In some instances, we need to view whatever we are experiencing from an objective perspective. This is where we need to go outside of ourselves. Here we get to examine our motives. We ask the question, 'Is this something I want, or something I need?'

> #ElevateNOW: Remember the one superpower we all have. We all have 100% control of the choices we make. Choose according to your inner champion.

If you are still not clear as to what your inner champion looks like, ask yourself the following question, 'The person I wish to become—what would they do in this situation?' We can all form an image of who we would like to be. Guess what? You are not so far away from that image if you really get present to who you are. The more you align your choices and behaviors to the person you wish to become, the more you make this person a reality. Remember, this is who you are anyway. You just need to be that person more consistently. How do you do that?

Beaming Down to Earth:

1. What are the things you think you need to feel whole? List them on paper and then challenge yourself to assess whether you really need them to see yourself as whole.
2. What is your strength(s)? How can this/these promote a steadier self-image?
3. What does your comparison behavior look like? Now think of all the possible things you don't know are happening behind the scenes. Is your comparison reflective of objective reality?
4. What are the external things you typically run toward to feel better about yourself? Which of them are needs and which of them are wants?

My desire is that you have now gotten your stories straight about who you are. We all have this inner victimizer deep down, who operates on fear and makes us feel like a piece of sh*t. We need to get to knowing we already have everything we need; we just need to access it. We move toward less comparing and more equalizing by knowing there's more to everyone's story than meets the eye (remember, they have an inner victimizer as well). You are not broken, my friend, and there is nothing about you that needs to be fixed. There are many things we could change about how we navigate in the world. And, as you press 'add to cart' on Amazon, always remember you don't need anything outside yourself to feel better.

Now that we have a better understanding of who we are, let's move toward love. What's love got to do with it? Well, plenty, in our next chapter, *What is love? Baby, don't hurt me. Don't hurt me, no more . . .*

CHAPTER TWO

Love: What Is Love? Baby, Don't Hurt Me. Don't Hurt Me, No More . . .

"I love love. Every day of my life is Valentine's Day.
When you're a pathological narcissist, you have to
fall in love with yourself every day." - Katya

One of my favorite lines from *A Course in Miracles* is, 'Only love is real'. Yet, how can love be the only thing that is real when we just went through a pseudo-apocalypse-like coronavirus? The need for work, money, face masks—that sh*t was real. We weren't just thinking about love, but about survival. How can we see only love as real when individuals we loved died of this mysterious virus so randomly and without reason? Even before the coronavirus pandemic, transgender women of color were being murdered on a regular basis, and still are. Hate groups defied laws to attack minority groups. Let's take it down to a more micro level: livelihoods were taken away in a second because of lockdown. 'Only love is real' was replaced with 'only this electricity bill is real'. How can we practice 'only love is real' when faced with so much uncertainty, as well as hate, in the world?

I remember Marianne Williamson saying in a lecture one time, "We can have love for someone like Hitler. We can have that brotherly love as a human being and not love the actions." This struck as quite the game-changer for me. This is where love can be very targeted. In my personal history, I have been screwed over many times, and sometimes profoundly. I have been raped.

I have been betrayed deeply by family members and loved ones. How can I love them when they committed the worst atrocities you can commit against a person?

If we remember the inner victimizer, this is the culmination of all the fear and trauma we have collected over our lifetimes. This is the force that governs the most heinous acts, and even the smaller crap we have done and may still do. If we see people as evil and hateful, of course "only love is real" seems impossible. Yet, if we can learn to separate the person from the act, we can do what Ms. Williamson is referring to. Why would anyone suggest an atrocity such as loving someone like Hitler?

#ElevateNow: We can love any person—yes, anyone—and not approve of/condone their actions.

As we will explore in the next chapter, negative emotions, when not managed effectively, are real energy suckers. When we engage in any kind of extended hate, anger, rage, you name it, we are literally not the person we want to be (especially if you picked up this book and you're already on the second chapter). If that is indeed the case, I know you do not want to be that negative b*tch the hatred/anger/rage will eventually turn you into.

Disclaimer: I am in no way, shape, or form suggesting we condone anyone's actions if they are hateful or hurtful. I am merely suggesting we separate the person from the actions to create more space for love in our lives and not let the negative feelings towards that person overtake us.

Think of someone right now whom you cannot fathom the thought of loving. When you think about this person and feel the negative emotions, how does this make you feel? Does it motivate you to do anything? Sure, there is an inherent benefit in the 'I'll show you' when we hate someone, like losing weight and scoring dates to 'show' your ex what's up, but if that remains the only source of motivation for your health and fitness, you in danger, Molly. It's like something you might hear at a twelve-step meeting, "It doesn't matter what got you here. What matters is what keeps you here." The distinction I want to make is our hate (or any other negative emotion) towards someone(s) can drive us to do something positive for ourselves, but it should never remain the reason why we do this action for the rest of our lives.

> **#ElevateNow: At some point, what we do for ourselves needs to come from a space of love, solely.**

But why do we have such difficulty turning away from hating someone? The main reason is because we have been taught, and I will go so far as to say programmed, that love will make us weak. If I let go of this anger towards so-and-so, they will be able to do that to me again, or people will think I am a wimp for not hating them like everyone else does. Love is really all about the acknowledgement of our connection as fellow human beings. Love can be as simple as that.

> **#ElevateNOW: Love does not make you weak. It makes you better.**

Many of us have also been taught/programmed to believe love will make us vulnerable to hurt, and therefore weak. Listen, so do fear, hatred . . . No emotion is exempt from making us vulnerable. It just hurts more when it's love that makes us vulnerable and someone uses that to hurt us. Hurt is part of the normal, average, and sometimes daily, human experience. No matter what we do, we will never escape being hurt. Here is our choice: we can live in anything but love, feel 'empowered', and be a bunch of bitter b*tches. OR, we can love, get hurt, work through the hurt, and come out stronger on the other side. For me, this is the biggest reason why 'only love is real'.

#ElevateNOW: Only love is real because it is the one and only emotion that truly makes us stronger and better people. No other emotion but love can do that.

I want to throw in some caution about using love inappropriately, which can happen. Many folks in the spiritual community will use love to bypass anything negative (more on bypassing in subsequent chapters). This is one of the things that I feel turn most people away from seeking spirituality. We see how it is used by many to shame others for having negative emotions (more of the need for negative emotions in the next chapter).

You don't have to announce it to the world either. This is about you and your enlightenment. To truly love someone(s), you do not need to make a big deal about it publicly.

Loving others only means you change the way you think about them and act around them. By change, I am referring to not being a shady b*tch because they are buttholes. It means treating them with 'brotherly' love, which can be as simple as kindness and respect. I think this is another turn-off for folks—believing they have to act all lovey-dovey. It's all a matter of you feeling love no matter what, because this is the person you want to be, independent of other people's actions. Be loving above all else, regardless of what the other person(s) are doing.

#ElevateNow: Love is more of a gift to yourself than it is to the other person(s).

Now that we are on the subject of loving yourself, let's turn our attention to the ever-elusive self-love. Living alone and being quarantined alone (well, with a twelve-year-old diabetic cat), I learned to love myself to a greater extent because of the simple fact that I was walking around my apartment with a mirror held up to me all the time. I am not much of a news show watcher, so when I wasn't having virtual sessions with my clients, I was in my own thoughts. This time gave me the opportunity to take a real HARD and OBJECTIVE look at myself during the eternal-feeling quarantine.

We were not born with low self-esteem. This is something that was given to us, whether maliciously or not, throughout our very formative years. This was the time when we absorbed anything that came our way. We did not have the wherewithal to discern what was right and wrong for us to internalize. We internalized everything and this is what created that pesky inner victimizer. The one that reminds us of how horrible we are on a daily basis based on this information we ingested when we weren't even old enough to think twice about it. This is tantamount to programming. And the same way we were programmed, we can reprogram our operating system to a new, improved version without losing all the wonderful features we already have.

> #ElevateNOW: Our first task in loving ourselves is to reprogram all the faulty systems we were given and own our inner champion while building ourselves stronger.

So, who is this inner champion I keep referring to? Everyone has someone who loves them. While you may think this has to do with genetic ties (in some cases, true), let's look at these people in your life, even if it's just one person. What do they love about you? Somehow, that one quality (or many) is part of your inner

19

champion, the *you* that is immutable and invincible. This is what makes you *you* and no one else. When we are in the throes of low self-esteem (especially after experiencing horrific traumas), it's hard to think of any part of us that can be loved. Well, there is.

> #ElevateNOW: Even if there is only one positive trait of your inner champion that you can identify and double down on, you have won and are on the road to loving yourself more.

Our inner champion has less to do with our external being than our internal being. We can change our exterior, and yes, you can change the interior. If there is something about yourself that you don't like physically/externally, ask yourself this question, 'Is this something I can change?' Yes? Then make a plan of action and take the next right step. If your answer is no, then how can you accept this and create greater self-love?

> #ElevateNOW: Acceptance is not mere passivity. It is the active acknowledgment that I will be okay with something and not let it affect my way of being, whether I like it or not.

We can accept something—still not approve of it—and live our best lives. Yet, if we don't accept or approve, we will be miserable sacks of sh*t. There are many things in our lives we can't change. We can't change our height (although a pair of fierce high heels or platform shoes could change that artificially). Things like height are genetically encoded in us. What we can change are things like weight, mental state, employment, relationship status, etc. We may THINK we can't change it, yet if we really look at the situation, the reason we tell ourselves we can't, is because the next steps are scary. We will talk more about fear in the next chapter and how to overcome this particular fear. Remember, folks, loving yourself can be very scary at first but it becomes the most amazing gift you can give to yourself, and to others as well.

> **#ElevateNOW: Surrender to who you ARE, not who you or others think you are supposed to be.**

Sometimes, the best way to surrender to who we are is as simple as changing the words in our self-talk. I remember a former therapist of mine asked me to keep track of all the times I said something negative about myself. That count was no joke. I treated myself like absolute sh*t just in the things I said to myself. If someone said the things to a loved one that I said to myself, I would beat their ass for being so mean (not really, as I am not much of a fighter, but you get my point). If using more positive self-talk seems daunting, use neutral statements. It can be something as simple as, 'I am okay.'

You can love yourself even if the most horrific of things have happened to you. I will not engage in a very popular spiritual dialogue of, 'Things don't happen to you; they happen for you'. That sh*t happened and it hurts and it carries so much weight. We have grown to literally hate and blame ourselves (and perhaps others as well) for these things. My inner champion, despite being bullied, raped, betrayed, etc., was always drawn to the imagery of the Phoenix from the *X-Men* comic books. Upon doing some research in the library (yes, I am that old), I found that the legend of the Phoenix has existed for hundreds of years. It speaks to a bird of fire. Only one of these birds exists at any given time. And when it is time for the bird to die, the new one is born from the ashes of the old.

This also spoke so strongly to me and I feel that I have risen from the ashes of the old me several times in my life. Part of my inner champion is overcoming any adversity that comes my way and rising stronger and brighter, like the Phoenix. This is the one thing I love about myself the most. This allows for transforming any atrocity in my life into (eventually) the greatest gift I can give to myself.

> #ElevateNOW: "If you can't love yourself, how in the hell are you going to love somebody else? Can I get an amen up in here?" – RuPaul

Beaming Down to Earth:

1. Pick one person for whom you have no love. Ask yourself: how can I separate the person from their actions? What would love towards them look like now?
2. In what ways do hate or any other negative feelings harm you? What would your best life look like if you loosened your grip on that hate/negative feeling and loved the person while not approving of their actions?
3. What is one quality you love about yourself (something internal, not external)? If you can't think of one, ask someone you love and trust. Know this is a quality of your inner champion and triple down on this strength while ignoring the weaknesses.
4. What are the common negative words/self-talk you use on a regular basis? How can you change them to be, at the very least, neutral?

Do we now know everything about love after reading this chapter? Hell, no. *A Course in Miracles* says, 'The course does not aim at teaching the meaning of love, for that is beyond what can be taught. It does aim, however, at removing the blocks to the awareness of love's presence, which is your natural inheritance'. This is a lifelong journey, folks, one I have barely even scratched the surface of. I am excited to explore more. We can start by taking in the guidance in this chapter. We can love anyone—yes, anyone—but not approve of what they have done and/or do. While this is a bitter pill to swallow, think of the alternative, which is a lifetime of hate and bitterness. We did not arrive in this world hating ourselves. It was a culmination of events that programmed us to feel this way about ourselves. We need to upgrade our programming and show the world who we really are.

Guess what? Some people already do know. Time for you to know this about yourself and one simple way is just to change the words in your self-dialogue. This will start you well on the way to loving yourself—and others—more.

Now, let's go to love's mortal enemy in *Fear: False Evidence . . . F*ck That, It Feels Real.*

CHAPTER THREE

Fear: False Evidence . . . F*ck That, It Feels Real

"Not today, Satan. Not today." Bianca Del Rio

With my extensive background in substance abuse and as a friend of Bill W. myself, I tend to quote twelve-step philosophy quite a bit. They have this really great saying about fear and what FEAR stands for: False Evidence Appearing Real. This is very pretty, but when I was having fevers and body aches as well as loss of sense of taste and smell at the end of March 2020, there was some real evidence to be scared. I was most concerned for who would take care of my cat (the ongoing care and treatment for his diabetes is costly) if something happened to me. These fears were real. They felt real. But were they really real?

The inner victimizer thrives on fear. Any hint of fear causes the inner victimizer to rouse from its slumber. It then stomps around in your inner psyche and gives you more fear to feed your present fear so that its appetite is satisfied. It's a never-ending cycle of torture. International drag queen superstar RuPaul likes to use the term 'inner saboteur' and makes reference to all of us having an inner saboteur. *A Course in Miracles* refers to fear as a false creation of the ego mind—our human mind—as opposed to our inner champion. If you really think about it, fear is very primal. Most mammals experience fear at some level (more on this in a bit). Let's bring this down for a second to some street-level understanding.

There are two kinds of fear: objective fear and subjective fear. The easiest way to differentiate between the two is as follows: objective fear occurs when your physical being may possibly be harmed. Think of a car barreling toward you, or someone pointing a gun to your head, or experiencing symptoms of coronavirus but you live alone and are not sick enough to go to the emergency room. These are all fears that anyone will agree are real. Folks who experience symptoms associated with PTSD, or who have been formally diagnosed with PTSD, have either experienced an event or witnessed an event that threatened physical integrity. This all boils down to a fear that just about anyone can see, even if they are not the victim.

Subjective fear is one that only the person feeling it will experience. No outside observer can objectively see what they are subjectively seeing and/or feeling. This will include things such as making a mistake at work and fearing losing your job. Or your partner hasn't called in over X amount of time and you fear they are cheating on you or about to break up with you. You think you are going to die from coronavirus and so will your diabetic cat because no one else wants that financial responsibility. As real as these fears feel, they are not real.

Subjective fears feel real because they not only get fed by the inner victimizer, but they activate most of your bodily systems to a higher level. It can involve the muscular, respiratory, and/or cardiovascular systems. This is why it is so easy to feel fear and fall back into a pattern of allowing fear to run rampant. It literally is the default setting in most mammals, just like a physical knee-jerk reaction. The key here is to know that it feels real because your body is now activated, thus giving us the illusion that it is real. To make matters worse, the inner victimizer/inner saboteur/ego mind doesn't help provide any support through this fear. On the contrary, it feeds you more and gets off on the process.

I don't want to encourage you to minimize your feelings in any
way. In my work with clients, I remind them to honor all their
feelings. We need to take that to the next level and shift from it
feeling real to engaging your inner champion into more objective
(reality-based) thinking. How the hell do we do that in the midst
of this? Well, we engage by taking control of our breathing and
taking control of our thoughts by looking for the physical
evidence to the contrary of what your inner victimizer/inner
saboteur/ego mind is saying. I used the terms subjective and
objective very strategically for this reason.

When trying to work through a subjective fear, you need to
engage objective thinking, feeling, and doing. I've worked with
clients with PTSD, having them work through a flashback by
orienting themselves to where they are now alleviates some of
the symptoms. Fear of losing your job? Breathe and remind
yourself of the value you bring to your job. Scared your partner
is cheating on you? Breathe and search for evidence beyond a
shadow of a doubt (just like *Law and Order*) to back this fear up.
Fear you may die? Guess what, Mary? It's going to happen to all
of us. So, instead of focusing on the fact that you may be dying,
focus on living your best life right here, right now. (This is not
to take away from individuals who are experiencing a life-threat-
ening illness diagnosed by a medical professional, or people
showing very real symptoms but have not yet seen a medical
professional, as was the case for me when I thought I had
COVID-19.) In the face of a diagnosis and/or symptoms, fear of
dying is very real. This is both a subjective and an objective fear.
Instead of focusing solely on the dying part, share some of the
focus on the living right here, right now part as well). Objective

fears are about the immediate future. Subjective fears are about a projected future.

> **#ElevateNOW: You cannot feel subjective fear if you are anchored into the present moment. Focusing on your breath is the easiest way to do so.**

Let's go back to how our fears as humans differ from those experienced by 'lower' life forms (I use quotations for 'lower', as sometimes they are way smarter and savvier than we are). One of the things that differentiate us from other animals is something we humans possess called a frontal lobe. It is that part of the brain that controls problem solving, decision making, labeling, planning, and many other higher-order mental processes that mammals without a frontal lobe can't do. Here's the deal: while we need a frontal lobe to not turn into hedonistic bastards, we can't shut it off either. Therefore, when we have that one thought (fed to us by the inner victimizer/inner saboteur/ego mind), our frontal lobe starts to work overtime. This fuels that initial thought of fear, and all of a sudden we think we are dying at 2a.m. just because we have a headache that won't go away.

I live in a busy bus/train area of town. One Sunday, my cat Logan was playing with a toy in the bed. A bus came by and made quite the ruckus. Logan stood up on all fours and stayed very still, eyes wide open. When the bus went on its way, Logan resumed what he was doing. We can learn a lot from Logan. Feel whatever feeling you are experiencing; don't add to it by thinking a bus is about to careen into the building. Don't judge yourself for feeling fear and go back to playing with your catnip toy.

You may be thinking, 'I do not like fear'. Well, duh! Who likes it other than the inner victimizer? While I do dislike feeling fear, I recognize its inherent value in our lives. If we subscribe to fear being a primal response to our world, then to some degree, it is part of our DNA. However, fear is one of those emotions we dislike the most. Why would we need it genetically? In lower-order behaviors, actions that nonhuman mammals engage in, we need to feel fear to survive. When we are in a situation unfamiliar to us, we need fear to heighten our level of awareness to our surroundings, just in case. It's a simple way of seeing how fear is quite useful, and necessary for our survival. In higher-order actions, those involving that frontal lobe, fear can arise in certain situations we may think of (sometimes fed by the inner victimizer) but we decide not to engage in said action because we are scared of the consequences. If used and managed appropriately, fear can make us better people. I use the term 'managed' with intent.

Let's say we are in a new neighborhood. We are not familiar with the surroundings. We will have that very basic fear of getting lost or possibly encountering questionable people. This fear will have us navigating the streets with more mindful intention.

Here is a different scenario with more frontal lobe functioning. Fear would be involved those times we would want to exact our revenge on someone who has wronged us. While that very primal rage is getting off on our plot, the frontal lobe will kick in and provide 134 worst-case-scenario conclusions of your act of revenge versus the one result you would want. You finally cancel the plans because you don't want to suffer the consequences.

> **#ElevateNOW: Fear is a necessary component of our lives that helps us survive in the physical realm as we grow mentally, emotionally, and spiritually.**

Well, damn, that's a big statement to make. We have to remember that when it comes to any emotion, once we are able to work through the primary emotions, we have more control of the secondary emotions. Psychologists argue whether or not there are four to six primary emotions (happiness, sadness, fear, disgust, anger, and surprise) while most spiritual philosophies will say there are only two (love and fear). I would agree with the spiritual idea, as all of what we consider to be positive emotions stem from love, and all of the emotions we consider as negative stem from fear. What is anxiety but fear of the future? Then, panic is having anxiety about being anxious. So, you see how they build upon each other.

> **#ElevateNOW: The key to using fear to your advantage is to manage it, not eliminate it.**

The one affirmation I have read in both psychological and spiritual texts has been, 'That which you resist, persists'. It's like the old saying, 'Don't think of a pink elephant'. What are you thinking of? A pink elephant. Our strongest tool at all levels is to never attempt to eliminate or medicate a negative feeling. Telling yourself, 'I shouldn't be scared. I don't want to be scared' is just going to turn your focus on the fear and make it grow. (Side note: don't let other people tell you how to feel either. Those who do are d*cks, for sure.) Feelings do not apply to logic like math and science do. Therefore, do not apply the logic of right or wrong to them. Feelings just are, and if we make them that objective, this is how we manage them, including fear.

I have referred in my past books to my three Cs to solving anything, but will repeat them briefly here to illustrate managing fear instead of getting invested in it.

- **Create awareness**, the first C, prompts us to create awareness of what we are feeling by simply naming it.

- **Compassionate witness** allows us to see the feeling from an objective, not subjective, perspective, which allows us to not engage with it and not increase the intensity of the feeling.
- **Choose differently**, the third C, gets us into our greatest superpower: choice. I can't always choose what I am feeling, but I can choose what I do about it 100% of the time.

When we get sick and tired of being scared all the time, it can give us the proper motivation to do something about it and emerge stronger. As an example, I fear rejection from what I perceive from guys who are in better shape than me. The inner victimizer would tell me finding the perfect partner could never happen because I don't have the stereotypical gay male body (you know the type I am referring to). There came a time when I said, "You know what? F*ck this fear!" This led to me swiping right, or tapping, or woofing at "better-looking" guys on the various apps on my phone. I walked into the fear to emerge stronger. Sure, Channing Tatum would intimidate the hell out of me (some of you were wondering when he would come up) but you best believe that I would flirt with him in person unapologetically. The only way to truly conquer a fear is to go right through it—not go around it, not walk away from it—but go right through it. A fear will continue to trigger you unless you want to do something about it and go right through it.

The other thing about fear is that it has been weaponized by religious institutions and the spiritual community. Using a fear to control and manipulate can be quite easy based on our intolerance of fear. Oxymoron, no? If you are a leader of an organization, like a church or movement, instilling fear into your audience would be a perfect way to get them to keep being your followers, as long as you make them some sort of promise of freedom from that fear, which usually takes the form of, 'Do this and you will no longer be scared. If you don't do this, you will continue to be scared (or you are damned)'. With the Catholic

Church, I experienced this firsthand. With the spiritual community, I most definitely experienced that. Later chapters will focus more deeply on this manipulation tactic. Rest assured, if you do not find a way to manage the fears that can't be conquered and conquer the fears that can be, you will fall prey to the next trendy (or even established) spiritual movement.

> #ElevateNOW: Once we recognize how our
> fears work on a personal level, we will become
> so enlightened and create our best lives.

Never, ever try to bypass your fear. Make room for it to CO-EXIST within your glorious self. Many of our day-to-day fears are easily manageable and once you get the hang of it, you will be able to walk into a room as if you were the Dalai Lama. He really is Enlightened as Hell, no?

When you start to feel scared about a goal you really want to achieve, fear will strike by making you think the end result(s) is too big or unattainable, or maybe you fear you can't do it. Here is where you get that king-size Snickers bar and break it down to those cute bite-size Snickers bars you get for Halloween because they can't possibly be as fattening, even if you eat 10 of them. Sure, have a picture in mind of what you want as the end result. Then break it down into manageable chunks. Once you have done that, you just focus on the next right step, no matter how small that step is. Your goal is to continually take the next right step towards the goal. (It doesn't have to be daily, just consistent.)

> #ElevateNOW: Every time the voice of fear
> of the future strikes, why go there?

This will be your most powerful tool to manage your fears. When that inner victimizer in the basement shouts to you all of the worst-case scenarios that could happen, tell the inner victimizer, 'Why go there?' We may not be in control of this inner victimizer nor of our primary emotions, but we have control over not jumping into the future. There is no point in doing so. Any great, genuine spiritual leader will tell you to stay in the here and now. Twelve-step programs all have the motto of 'one day at a time'. The reality is that at the start, most things have a 50% chance of failing and 50% chance of succeeding. Guess who is in charge of these percentiles after you get off the starting line? You, my little gurus. So, ask yourself again: why go there?

Beaming Down to Earth:

1. Make a list of all your fears. Now separate them into two columns: objective and subjective. Which list has the greater number of fears?
2. What is one of your biggest fears? Now, by doing some compassionate witnessing, how can this fear be turned into a pathway for personal growth? Hint: they all can be used for that purpose if we get objective and creative enough.
3. What are the common fear-provoking statements the inner victimizer makes that increase your fears? Let's reframe them to decrease the power of those initial thoughts.
4. Pick a goal you want to achieve without having any active intention of fulfilling it right now. Break this goal down to small steps. Really small, if you have to. What's the first step?

Fear feels like our biggest enemy, yet it can be an asset. Feelings are never right or wrong, as they are beyond the scope of logic. They just are. We all experience fears, ALL OF US. All fears can be broken down into two types: the kind that threaten your physical existence, and those that are self-created (with the help of the inner victimizer). If we get to know how fear impacts us as individuals, we will be better suited to manage our fears with the ease of an enlightened guru and use them for our personal growth and development. Staying in the present moment is our greatest tool to manage fears and we can assist this mindful state of mind by breaking things down into small bits that we can manage at a single time.

Understanding fear seems to be the perfect segue into talking about something that strikes fear in all of us in *Chapter Four: Forgiveness: Payback Is Not a Bi*ch, But Your Ex Won't Stop Stalking You Online.*

CHAPTER FOUR

Forgiveness: Payback Is Not a B*tch, But Your Ex Won't Stop Stalking You Online

"Don't get bitter. Just get better." - Alyssa Edwards

I recall from my upbringing that forgiveness was a requirement of being a good Catholic. We went to confession on a regular basis to be absolved of our sins. We would be instructed to 'sin no more', yet all I wanted was to lust over my high school freshman-year crush, Matthew. I mean, I was a gay kid who went to an all-boy Catholic school and we were made to shower after physical education. My eyes sinned like no tomorrow. I never felt empowered after confession, either. I actually felt more fear than anything else, as inevitably, I was going to commit the same sin again. The perpetual cycle of sinning and confessing just started to lose its meaning altogether.

The church was quite adamant about forgiving others. This was all well and good, but having been the victim of horrific bullying for many years, as well as a rape at the age of 15, how was I to forgive others? Forgiveness was kind of difficult when I looked at the bruises or realized that my first sexual experience with a man was forced upon me. These experiences left me broken for many years. The thought of forgiving my abusers made me feel weaker than I already felt. Also, how did I forgive myself for allowing these things to happen? Catholicism did not offer any way that made sense.

A side note about Catholicism and traditional Judeo Christian beliefs: the Bible states that Jesus instructs us to turn the other cheek. Jesus never really said what to do afterwards, did he?

During my time in twelve-step fellowships, religion was out the window. There was no need to confess anything. While working a fourth and fifth step, the recovering person worked through their past by making 'a searching and fearless moral inventory' and later, they 'admitted to God, to ourselves, and to another human being the exact nature of our wrongs'. This concept was quite novel for me, as I didn't necessarily have to confess my sins (as that had lost all meaning by then). This concept of exact nature is very empowering as it shifts away from a *mea culpa* victimization to an attitude of enlightenment about what we need to do differently. It was less about wrongness and more about learning about yourself and what you did. Such a departure from what I was exposed to in my upbringing.

This is built upon with the 10th step, in which the recovering person continues to take personal inventory and when they were wrong, promptly admitted it. This is mostly done via daily inventory of some sort, such as journaling. If done correctly, the 10th step allows the recovering person to be empowered about where they went wrong, which creates the insight to do it differently next time. Many popular guided journals will prompt the user to identify how they could have made today better, much like the 10th step does.

Twelve-step groups have this great saying about resentments, which is essentially a lack of forgiveness. It goes, 'Resentments are like me drinking poison, expecting you to die'. When I hold a resentment, the only one impacted is me. I seethe in this anger and hatred and bitterness and the other person is just skipping along the Yellow Brick Road, oblivious to the various times I wished a plague of locusts on them. Well, sh*t, if that doesn't drive the point home of the need to forgive others and let go, I don't know what else does.

Now, the spiritual community I used to belong to made forgiveness almost like a requirement again. You mean I did all this work to leave the Catholic faith only to be surrounded by a bunch of Karens telling me I had to forgive? I have experienced a lot of shaming by so-called spiritual people to do things exactly how they do them, including forgiveness, and if you don't, they turn into Mean Girls and shun you.

Any good, spiritual belief needs to empower the believer. Thanks to Jack Kornfield, an American author, Buddhist monk, and clinical psychologist, I stumbled upon a concept of forgiveness that finally worked for me.

> **#ElevateNOW: Forgiveness means I acknowledge something went wrong in the past and I make an active choice today to not let it impact my present and future.**

This is the most empowering and inclusive concept of forgiveness I have ever seen. First, it's empowering without any need for blame/self-blame. You are just acknowledging (stating what is evident) what went wrong. The second part forces you to make a choice on how you want to live your life. Applying this to my abusers of the past, I can definitely acknowledge that something went wrong and then I choose to not be in a victim state of mind. With the appropriate help (professional mental health services), I can make peace with it and choose to be a survivor instead of a victim. I was a victim at the time of the abuse. I made myself a victim for many years after because I didn't know what to do. Today, I am a survivor. I don't even need to forgive (in the traditional use of the word) my abusers. I am acknowledging what happened yesterday and choose who I am today. Today, I get to choose to be either a victim or a survivor through this concept of forgiveness.

As this would apply to forgiving yourself, I will share with you something that is going to blow your mind. The word 'sin' comes from the Greek word *Hamartia*. This is an archery term meaning 'to miss the mark'. Again, we find a way to make something historically disempowering into something that can make you feel like Superman or Wonder Woman. When I have made errors in the past, I would beat myself up mercilessly. I would make myself wrong. With this definition of sin, the definition of missing the mark, I can certainly be angry at myself, yet know that I simply missed the mark and I can work towards either getting closer to the mark or hitting the mark next time. I did something that was not in agreement with who I want to be, so I take the next right steps.

#ElevateNOW: When I sin, I am doing something that is not in alignment with my inner champion and I can take action to do better next time.

Why is a discussion on forgiveness so important? Because enlightenment really involves walking through our lives as the best possible version of ourselves at any given time, having authentic connections with others, and freeing up any barriers towards these connections. If you think about it, forgiveness is a gift we give ourselves, really. If the forgiveness is directed at another person, they don't even have to know. Forgiveness is a choice you make for yourself and no one else.

My ex-boyfriend broke up with me in 2016. I went on my path, separate from him, because the further I was from him, the more I realized what a narcissist he is. He would spy on my social media and even send mutual acquaintances to find out information about me. He went so far as to send his current boyfriend to ask me to come back into his life "because he didn't like when people didn't forgive him." Little did he know that I had long

38

ago forgiven him. I just made a choice to never have him in my life in any capacity because he didn't and couldn't add anything positive to who I am today. Bye, girl, bye.

> **#ElevateNOW: You can forgive someone and not have them in your life if you don't choose to. Forgiveness and friendship can be mutually exclusive.**

Some people will say this is not forgiveness, yet let's cut to the chase. You acknowledge that something went wrong, you make an active choice to do better today, and you try to get closer to the mark. Why would you need someone, who doesn't contribute anything positive, to be in your life today? Despite what some religions and cultures would say (and as a Latino person, what I just said is very counterculture), forgiveness is all about you and nothing to do with them. It's all about making the best choices for you to move forward. NO amount of shaming will ever convince me to let someone who abused me back in. This isn't said out of fear of the abuse happening again. This is said in direct connection to who I want to be today and what I want my life to look like today. No anger or resentment. Just a choice.

Sometimes, however, being away from the person may not always be an option. (I hope that no one reading this is in a domestic situation in which you fear leaving because you are being physically assaulted or threatened in some capacity. If you are, please contact the National Domestic Violence Hotline at 1-800-799-7233 or https://www.nationaldahelpline.org.uk in the United States or https://www.refuge.org.uk/get-help-now/phone-the-helpline/ in the UK).

Everything I have mentioned so far can also be applied to a situation in which you may not want to walk away from the person who hurt you. How can you move on and feel free?

Our previous discussion on the frontal lobe will remind you of the part of the brain where we label stuff. This is the inner victimizer's most formidable weapon. Remember, the inner victimizer is the culmination of your lifelong fears, resentments, anxieties, and traumas, who resides within us and wants us miserable. We fear forgiveness could open the door for the person to do the same thing again (or worse). We hold on to unforgiveness as a shield to protect us from future harm. This shield works both ways, though. There is no way for this shield to only work for your sole benefit.

While we block potential future harm with unforgiveness, this also creates a block in our enlightenment. While you are getting ready for something that is only potential (and face it, another human hurting us is always a potential), you block your ability to connect with others. This fear of getting hurt is not limited to the person in question. You will start to question other people's intentions as well. You stop your progression and evolution to the person you want to be. There is the block.

Let's say your romantic partner or business partner did something very hurtful to you. This is not a situation that you would (or could) leave the partnership for, yet you are still in pain over what they did. Acknowledge what went wrong, but in an objective fashion. The easiest way to do that is to not add "to me" to the end of the acknowledgement (i.e., he/she did this to me). Simply state what went wrong. Objectively, can you own any part in this? No need for self-flagellation either. Just a simple statement of fact. Can this situation be rectified somehow? If so, take the steps to do so. If not, then ask yourself the hard question,

'Can I live with this and still feel an authentic connection with this person?'

Even in a situation with a partner, your best course of action is to choose if you are going to let this situation block you from your own growth by withholding forgiveness. The answer may be leaving the partnership behind. This is ultimately your choice. Make the choice that is in alignment with whom you want to be. Forget how quickly you should forgive because this isn't a competition. This is you and you are the author of your own book. And remember, forgiving and allowing the person to stay in your life are not one and the same.

And the old adage of forgive *and* forget doesn't always ring true. This saying disempowers you from the word go, as it implies forgetting something that was so painful. Sorry, Mary, I can't forget the names of the boys who beat me in the seventh grade or the man who raped me when I was 15, no matter how hard I try. I have tried, believe me. I would change 'forget' to 'let go' (which we will talk about soon). By asking yourself the hard questions I just mentioned, you can then choose to let go. It's unrealistic to think you will forget. Forgiveness does not offer amnesia. It provides freedom to make the best choices for yourself.

> **#ElevateNOW: Forgiveness is not necessary because your inner champion cannot be harmed.**

To close this up, if we keep in mind the concept of our inner champion, we know this part of us cannot be harmed by anyone but us. Saying forgiveness is not necessary is not contradicting myself. Once we have mastered the ability to forgive by using these concepts, we get to the place in our lives where things won't sting us quite as hard. They will always sting, but we won't suffer like we used to.

41

I can tell you, as a rape trauma survivor and a survivor of relentless bullying over the course of many years, I have been able, in time, to overcome these atrocities and make myself stronger. I share my story to empower myself and others. At the time of the events, I was a victim. I remained a victim for many years because I could not forgive myself for not being able to stop it. Through much work on myself and the help of an amazing support system through the years, I am not a victim anymore. I am a winner, baby.

Beaming Down to Earth:

1. Pick one thing you have done for which you haven't forgiven yourself or are having difficulty forgiving yourself. How can you use the concept of sin (in the archery context) to see it differently?
2. Pick one thing someone else has done to you that you are having trouble forgiving. Now, see it from the lens of knowing your inner champion cannot be harmed. How does this situation change for you?
3. Think of a relationship or situation in which you have refused to practice forgiveness. What was your mental, emotional, physical, and spiritual state as a result of withholding? Did it empower you at all?
4. Is there someone in your life whom you have forgiven and allowed to stay in your life? Is this relationship working for you anymore?

When it comes to forgiveness, we need to drop a lot of the traditional stuff we learned so we can move into a space of authentic forgiveness. Whatever concept(s) work for you, make sure it is personal to you. With any spiritual/metaphysical belief, it should always empower you. If it drains you or makes you wrong, it's probably not the belief you should be following.

Now, my children, you are forgiven; go and sin no more. But seriously, I hope this chapter gives you the insight to forgive powerfully and still feel like a guru. Let's move on to our next step in being Enlightened as Hell with *Chapter Five: Letting Go: Let It Go, B*tch, Just Drop It Already.*

CHAPTER FIVE

Letting Go: Let It Go, B*tch, Just Drop It Already

"Now I'm the star, I'm shooting far, and you're a basic hun. I'm topping all the charts now, 'cause I'm number 4, 3, 2, 1." - Cheryl Hole

In 2013, we were blessed with the best Disney movie of all time: *Frozen*. We were also blessed with the song, *Let It Go*, as rendered by the indelible Idina Menzel. Now, while this movie may have been the bane of many parents' existences, it tells a very powerful tale about letting go and surrendering as well as unhealthy attachments to status quo and control. For those of you who have not seen the movie (shame on you), spoilers ahead.

Elsa was born with ice powers that were fun until she accidentally hurt her little sister. The sister was healed and Elsa was then told to conceal who she was and not allow her feelings to take over, as this could make her powers flare up. Gloves and her bedroom became her prison, living in isolation from those she loved. Elsa was an outsider due to her affliction; a status imposed upon her by her parents and her own inner victimizer in the basement. When her parents died, she was to assume the role of queen. At her coronation, she had to remove her gloves during the ceremony. At one point, she lost control of her emotions and her powers flared up. This led to her leaving her kingdom in shame and hiding away in the icy mountains. It wasn't until her sister's life was in jeopardy once again that Elsa fully accepted who she was and did indeed let go.

45

When talking about surrendering, I usually use Dorothy and *The Wizard of Oz* as an example. However, I've done that twice before and so many others have written about this too. Elsa seems like the next right choice, as I can relate to her more so than I can to Dorothy. Elsa was made to feel like there was something inherently wrong with her. Her parents told her, "conceal, don't feel." She hid from who she was for most of her life. When her secret was revealed, she ran away and hid some more. She refused any help, love, or support. She was convinced she would live the rest of her life alone, in hiding. She denied who she was because she thought she had to. Her inner victimizer even came to life at some point during the movie as a giant ice monster. This was my life before enlightenment—without the kingdom, ice powers, and amazing singing voice, of course. That was, until I surrendered to who I truly am and who others are as well.

> #ElevateNOW: One major key in becoming
> Enlightened as Hell is to surrender to our
> own greatness, as well as that of others.

We chatted previously about the notion of our inner champion. Surrendering and letting go is a major, and almost daily, part of getting to know that side of us. Throughout the day, we will want things to go a certain way. We make a commitment in the morning to just be the best possible version of ourselves we want to be. Then, BAM, something happens that derails our perfect plans. If we were at fault, we start to beat ourselves up. If someone else is to blame, we beat them up mentally. We forget our initial goal of having a kick-ass day and instead, kick our own ass or those of other people.

How about recognizing the human side to everyone, along

46

with the inner champion, to have a more balanced view of the world in general? This is where letting go of how things need to be and surrendering to how things actually are bring us closer to enlightenment each day. We are all on this journey together and we will all make mistakes along the way. Let it go and surrender to the present moment, exactly how it is.

I get it. We want what we want. This doesn't mean we can't have what we want. We need to be more flexible. Needing things to look a certain way and holding on to this idea for dear life is what causes us to lose our enlightened status. The Buddhists have what's called the Four Noble Truths. For me, the first two noble truths speak to the nature of surrendering and letting go. It basically says, 'Mary, all human life is suffering and the cause of that suffering is our attachment to things'. This is my very flippant, yet accurate, interpretation. The first thing to let go of is the thought that we will never suffer. I personally hate the word 'suffer' as it can be a tad dramatic in its usage, but let's go with it for now. Because we are human, because we have that pesky frontal lobe, and because the world is just the way it is, we will have negative experiences. There is no escaping this. Right here, we need to let go of the very maladaptive notion of bad things happening to good people. How about bad things just happen to anybody and everybody?

Now, where does suffering come in? By not accepting that bad sh*t is just going to happen and getting pissed that it did. This is the attachment Buddhists philosophize about. I can want something to be a certain way, but if I hold on too tightly to what I want, then I will suffer when it doesn't show up the way I was wanting it to. We fight the universe because something we didn't want showed up in our lives instead. We fight what's in front of us instead of letting go and surrendering to what's right in front of us (which most times is exactly what we need; we just don't realize it).

47

Time to quote another one of my favorite movie characters (now owned by Disney): Yoda. I could really just insert this quote and be done with this chapter. He stated, "Train yourself to let go of everything you fear to lose." Yoda is trying to tell us to loosen our grip on the things we want in life. The tighter we hold on, the greater the chances of losing what we want. There is also an inherent danger in losing what we already have with such a strong hold on what we want. Let's desire something, take the most appropriate steps towards making that happen, let go of what it needs to look like, surrender outcomes, and just stop fighting.

> **#ElevateNOW: Surrendering means I stop fighting myself, others, and the world.**

Why do we fight ourselves, others, and the universe at large? Here is a solemn truth that may cause you to want to throw this book out the window: we are control freaks. *Please read that again.* Every one of us has control issues. Even the meekest of individuals has control issues—they control others by their meekness. Part of us fears not getting what we want exactly how we want it because that will mean there is something inherently wrong with us, as the inner victimizer would have us believe. This is the furthest thing from owning who you are, as there is nothing wrong with us.

The other part of us fears how others perceive us. My internship supervisor used to call this 'impression management'. Since the inner victimizer has fed us so much false information about ourselves, we fear that others will find us out. They will be able to verify what we fear is true about ourselves. When that fear of being found out kicks in, we freak out and will start to want to, or actually try to, control everything around us to prevent this from happening.

#ElevateNOW: The most beautiful version
of you contains your strengths AND
flaws. Own them both equally.

Let's talk social media for a little bit. You can tell the fakes from authentic people almost right away. Besides being enlightened by owning your flaws authentically, it's also very sexy. Sure, this 'influencer' may have a kick-ass body and stunning looks, but if there are no flaws, where is the depth to their persona? Probably not on social media, as they spend more time preparing their posts to be just perfect as opposed to being real with their audience. They spend more time controlling how other people may perceive them than actually revealing who they are. Much like Elsa did in the first *Frozen* movie.

Another reason we love to control (and thereby not surrender and let go) is because we hate not knowing. Now for this part, I can bring in an amazing song from *Frozen 2: Into The Unknown*. During this song, Elsa hears someone or something calling to her, a voice no one else can hear, and she doesn't know what to do about it. She decides it's time to go into the unknown and figure this out. Many of us could benefit from having the guts Elsa had to follow this voice. Too many times I have heard my clients say something along the lines of, "But I don't know what is on the other side," or "What if I fail?" There is nothing enlightened about allowing fears of the future to prevent us from taking actions in our lives. It's totally fine and enlightened to feel the feelings. It's quite another to actively choose not to take a course of action based solely on not knowing the outcome.

We don't like what we don't know (unless we don't know that we don't know something). This is another part of the human condition. We also have to see the role that anxiety plays as well. Anxiety is always a future-based emotion. Anxiety is also one of

49

those full-body responses. Virtually every system in your body (muscular, cardiovascular, respiratory) becomes involved when anxiety is activated. We then engage in control strategies to alleviate the symptoms of anxiety. Oh, I don't know what the outcome is going to be? Well, then, I just won't do it. Anxiety resolved, and we are none the better for it.

#ElevateNOW: Life really happens in the unknowns.

Our biggest growth potential as human beings is being able to utilize all our superpowers when we are in the unknown. It takes little self-potential to do things when the outcome is sure or it's a safe venture. Much like our physical muscles, we will grow bigger and stronger as we let go of attachments and surrender outcomes. Our biggest weapon to make this happen? Choice. I do want to acknowledge that there are heinous acts committed on a person that really leave the victim with no choice. The act leaves them powerless and feeling powerless afterwards. These violent situations leave the victim with very little to no room to exercise their power of choice. My wish is that none of you readers are or were the victims of these atrocities. If you need them, please refer to the resources provided in Chapter Four.

This will be another concept I will repeat from previous writings as it is so important to remember. The only thing we ever have 100% control over 100% of the time are the choices we make. No matter what situation we are in, even if someone is pointing a gun to our heads, we always have a choice. You can choose to hand over what the assailant is asking for or you can choose to not do so. This situation may seem like you only have one choice but objectively, you do have two choices. Yes, in some instances the choice is quite obvious, but if you take a step back, the not-so-obvious choice is still a choice. When given this freedom, folks like to put up some resistance and say, "But I didn't have a choice." We always have, at the very least, two choices. It is built in, no matter what.

We can choose to hold on to what we want and leave nail marks on the door frame. Or we can choose to drop the need to have things a certain way. Imagine walking around your own life with no expectations from yourself and others (other than some of the common-courtesy ones, but even then, people can choose not to be so courteous). Just fantasize for a few moments about walking through life, free of needing to have things a certain way. Some of you will probably say you feel light and unencumbered. Some of you will say you're feeling abject terror. Which way of life are you wanting to choose right here, right now, for yourself?

Are we then to give up what we want? Nothing could be further from the truth. Drop the need (not want) for things to be your way all the time. Embrace the possibility of what could be within the realm of what you desire. My last relationship did not look anything like I would have initially wanted, but the end result was everything.

#ElevateNow: Make a decision to turn your will over to a power greater than yourself.

I can't talk about letting go and surrendering without a discussion on the Third Step. As stated in the literature, 'We made a decision to turn our will and our lives over to the care of God as we understood Him'. Yeah, I know, the word God is there (and also a male pronoun). Notice how it ends with 'how we understood Him'. The beauty of Twelve-Step programs is that God is not any one particular God. It is a power greater than yourself. This could take on many different forms for the person in recovery, and I will encourage you do to the same. Whatever serves as a power greater than yourself will work.

When we make a decision to turn our will and our lives over to a power greater than ourselves, this is the ultimate form of surrender. How it would look is simple: I identify what it is that I want. I take all the appropriate steps towards making this a reality. I then wait for my Higher Power/the Universe to do its thing. The steps are simple. The choice to not control the outcomes is the hardest part, not because it is so difficult but because it is so different.

The last tool I will share with you for surrendering and letting go are my timeless acceptance-versus-approval questions. Let's say there is something in our life we don't approve of. The question to ask is: can we change it? If we can, take the action. If it's something you can't change (i.e., height, eye color, genetics of some sort), what can you do to accept it? If we cannot approve of something, we can accept it and live in peace. However, if we don't approve and we don't accept, such as is the case with not surrendering and not letting go, we will be miserable.

To close off this chapter that was inspired by the *Frozen* movies, the final big Elsa song in the second movie is *Show Yourself*. It is a song about revealing who you really are and embracing everything about you, imperfections and all. One lyric always stood out to me:

"Show yourself. Step into your power. Throw yourself into something new. You are the one you've been waiting for all of your life. Show yourself."

Letting go of being in control of everything 24/7 is the truest way to show up for yourself and others.

Beaming Down to Earth:

1. When you are not sure of the results you may get or you are not getting the results you want, what can you tell yourself to move you into a state of loosening your grip?

2. What are the predominant feelings you experience when you are trying to control everything around you?
3. What have these feelings prevented you from achieving?
4. What could serve as a power greater than yourself to facilitate your enlightenment into surrendering and letting go?

By letting it go, you venture into the unknown and show yourself (and others) what a guru you really are. While it can be quite difficult to keep it together, especially when it's something you really want, is it worth making yourself absolutely insane trying to control all the variables? The steps to loosening your grip may seem hard, but only because it is not what you are used to doing. Take a chance and let it go.

You have now gone on this magic journey into freedom and enlightenment by letting go and surrendering. Feels great, no? Let's continue this journey with our next chapter: *Manifesting: The Law of Distraction.*

CHAPTER SIX

Manifesting: The Law of Distraction

"I just want fried chicken." - Juju Bee

When books like *The Secret* and *The Law of Attraction* first came out, I was pretty pumped. It was like real-life superhero stuff, and I was so ready. The teenager who devoured comic books was jumping for joy that he could now have superpowers. *The Secret* made me feel like Professor X from the *X-Men*, and *The Law of Attraction* seemed very Dr. Strange.

Before we get into that, if you were to look up the word 'manifest' in the dictionary, it would say something along the lines of, 'to display or show by your behaviors or appearance'. The word 'attract' comes from the Latin words *ad* (to) and *trahere* (draw). If you look at these words from this objective definition perspective, this is quite a departure from what you will see in the spiritual/self-help community. So, to manifest is to demonstrate, and attract is to draw in. A little bit different than what you see in popular self-help/spiritual books. (I am exempting anything written by Esther Hicks because she clearly is an enlightened being. Her followers are a bunch of di*ks.)

> **#ElevateNOW: You have to demonstrate who you are to draw in what you want.**

Two things prevented me from really grasping what the authors of *The Secret* and *The Law of Attraction* were teaching me: the d*cks who would translate these philosophies into their own snake-oil programs, and my not believing I could attract what I wanted in life.

I remember one encounter with a so-called spiritual coach on Facebook in which she wrote, 'Oh Tony, you shouldn't think that way because you will only attract more of that into your life'. Oh, so I can make myself fat just by thinking I am fat? By thinking only skinny thoughts, I will then lose weight? Minor backstory: I had never met her and she jumped on a comment I made on a friend's post of Facebook about the inauthenticity of spiritual coaches on Facebook. My point was made quite clearly in this interaction. Shaking my head does not describe what I was feeling. I may have caused a seizure with the force of the eye roll reading Spirit Karen's comment. One way 'manifesting' is translated very poorly (and to the translator's benefit) is the idea that you should not have any negative thoughts because you will only attract negativity into your life.

> #ElevateNOW: Manifesting is most potent
> with the acceptance of the presence of negative
> experiences, along with the mindful intention
> of creating something different for yourself.

It is utterly impossible to eliminate all negative experiences in human existence. That is not something you can manifest and the presence of negative experiences does not prevent you from manifesting. By embracing who we are as a whole—this includes all our strengths as well as weaknesses—we are in a more authentic state of being. The more we push away our negative experiences, the stronger these experiences will get or they will come out in a different fashion. This is a concept called bypassing, and bypassing has become very popular in the self-help/spiritual community.

Essentially, bypassing is using higher-order thinking and/or spiritual theories to sidestep negative experiences. It's like adding glitter to spoiled food and serving it as the main course. This is approaching life as two halves of a being: the half you want others and 'God' to know about and the half you are hiding. Ever think that using the negative stuff that has happened to you could *help* with manifesting?

We don't always know what we want. I will guarantee you that we know what we don't want. In my last relationship, I wrote down the qualities I wanted in a man. I totally got them, but where I missed the mark was not going deeper into what I wanted, and staying in the superficial. Once that relationship ended, I had a VERY clear idea of what I don't want. Therefore, in any attempts at dating, I will remember (not obsess over) what I don't want, as it will make what I do want clearer.

> #ElevateNOW: Knowing what you don't want is a very powerful tool in manifesting what you do want.

The first key in manifesting is your focus on what you don't want. But make this more of a recall and not one of regurgitating the past. The difference is that in recall, you simply remember something in a very matter-of-fact way. Regurgitating is more of an obsessive, self-victimization stance. You are reliving old negative experiences in a way that completely saps you of any ability to manifest. In fact, regurgitating will attract what you don't want because it's all you're going to see in the world.

You don't need to avoid negative experiences; you need to not relive it in your quest to manifest the life you want.

The second key in your manifesting is mindful intention. Take a look at your motives for doing something. As an example, while I would have loved for my first book to become a *New York Times* bestseller (it wasn't), my intention in writing my first book was to create a guide for loving yourself so much that your relationship status does not even become that important. I wanted to write a book I would want to read. If my mindful intention was to write a *NYT* bestseller, I don't know that I would have been quite as raw in writing it. My writing would have been more focused on what would make a *NYT* bestseller and not on writing a book I would want to read.

Check your motives any time you want to manifest something in your life.

> #ElevateNOW: Being fully aware of your motives for doing anything in your life will be key in its success.

In working with clients, I challenge them to look at their motives for doing anything, and I do that in pretty much every session. If your motive for being in a relationship is that it's time for you to share your life with someone in a meaningful way, you will show up for yourself and for your partner in full authenticity. If your motive for being in a relationship is to validate your existence and be like everyone else, you will be seeking (or in) a relationship from a space of incompleteness and fakeness. Can you make it work? Sure, but will it work to its fullest potential? To your fullest potential?

Your last step in manifesting is less about what you need to *do*. It's all about who you need to *be*. Most of the time in the self-help/spiritual community, it seems all you have to do is think. I can think constantly about a lot of things, and I do, yet thinking alone will not bring into my existence what I want to manifest. Think of it this way: it's less what do you need to *do* and more who do you need to *be* every day to manifest what you want and keep what you want. Using this mentality, we capture the essence of the definitions I provided earlier on manifest and attract. We demonstrate who we are to draw in what we want.

> **#ElevateNOW:** If you focus more on who you need to be and less on what you need to do, you will have much greater chances of manifesting what you want for your life.

Any time we achieve a goal, we can't then stop doing the work, right? The reason diets don't work is because most people will go back to their normal eating patterns once they have achieved their goal weight. So, if you shift your mindful intention from just action into more of a state of being, you will then be able to engage in the appropriate behaviors that will facilitate your maintaining what you have manifested.

> **#ElevateNOW:** Consistent mindful intention and being are your key practices in manifesting as well as in being enlightened.

There is nothing passive about attraction and manifesting. It is not just about thinking positive thoughts, which is super unrealistic. It is a very active position you are choosing to take in your life to create, draw in, and demonstrate what you want your life to be, and being consistent with this way of being. Simple in theory, but difficult in execution because it is so different from what we are used to. If you think about it, any new behavior will be difficult because it is so different, but with practice, it will become second nature.

There is one thought we do need to be wary of. This negative thought is thinking you can't attract/manifest something in your life. When we engage in this, we can be sure the inner victimizer is hard at work, roaring in its dwelling, making you feel less than, because you dared to have an idea to improve your life. This is where I usually use something that is said frequently in Twelve-Step meeting rooms, "Thank you for sharing and keep coming back."

If we start our path of manifesting and attracting by thinking we can't do it, of course we won't and it's not just because of our thoughts. These self-defeating thoughts will have a direct influence on our behaviors. There is a line from *A Course in Miracles* that I like: 'Only what you have not given can be lacking in any situation'. This line from the *Course* is in direct alignment with Law of Attraction philosophies.

> #ElevateNow: We need to fully embrace and
> become that which we want to manifest in
> our way of being, thinking, and doing.

The inner victimizer will feed us whatever thoughts it wants in order to make us miserable. What we always need to remember is that it is easier to behave/act into a new way of thinking than think into a new way of acting/behaving. When that inner victimizer's thoughts start to come up from our psyche, you must still act/behave in the way that is most in alignment to what you what you want to draw in. Acting/behaving first is easier than thinking yourself out of it. It's almost like walking away from an argument. You cut the effects of the argument by not being in the presence of it.

The negative thought of you not being able to manifest what you want in life is further complicated by what social media and self-help/spiritual gurus will show and tell you. The pun of show-and-tell is quite intended because it really does feel like people are showing you their best whatever to one-up others in the same field. This is where you want to be very mindful of your social media consumption, and notice if you're just unconsciously swallowing what gurus feed you.

Whatever course of action we take, even if it's the same actions someone else is taking, will inevitably give different results to different people. For example, not all size mediums will fit the same on me. My bicep exercise routine will not give me the same biceps as Channing Tatum. We can all be on the same path, yet get different results. It's great that this self-proclaimed money-manifesting guru is traveling the world, but what do you really want? If you are wanting their life, then we have to go back to your motives for what you want to manifest.

> #ElevateNOW: Whatever it is you are wanting to manifest in your life will look differently for you than for someone else. Rejoice in your individuality.

When you see a post or a video from a guru, see if what they suggest feels right to you; this then will be a good course of action. The way will be emotionally obstacle free. If the guru or group needs to give you a hard sell and you are feeling backed into a corner, get the hell out of there because, Mary, this is not for you. Manifesting and attracting need to feel empowering for you, not like it's sucking all the energy out of you or making you question yourself and possibly take out a second mortgage on your home to purchase a coaching program.

Going back to my girl, Marianne Williamson (and if you haven't caught on, I think she is Enlightened as Hell)—I remember her saying in one of her lectures something to the effect of "the problem with Law of Attraction is that it implies you are lacking something." She refers back to the *Course* by stating one of its basic tenets, which is that the only problem we have is our thoughts of separation from God (Higher Power). If we take what Marianne and the *Course* say into consideration, manifesting and attracting need to come from a state of wholeness and completeness.

> #ElevateNOW: When we approach manifesting
> and attraction from a state of adding to
> our lives and not filling a void in our lives,
> our success rate rises exponentially.

This will make or break your manifesting/attracting: what is it providing in your life? Completion or complementary addition? If you think about it, it brings together everything we have talked about in this chapter. Be honest with yourself. No one else needs to know.

Does all of this make you nervous or scare you? My last question to you in this chapter is, how badly do you want it? Another Twelve-Step philosophy, mainly Narcotics Anonymous, says, "You chase your recovery like you chased your drugs." Do all of the work to draw in what you want in your life fiercely and consistently.

Beaming Down to Earth:

1. Take note of the negative thoughts that surface when you think of manifesting/attracting something into your life. Are they blocking the manifestation/attraction or preventing you from taking action?
2. Think of something you may have manifested/attracted in the past but it showed up in a way you did not want. How

can this information help you get clearer on what you do want?

3. Generally speaking, what are your motives for engaging in any manifesting/attracting behavior? Are they to add to your life or to fill a perceived void in your life?

4. When you think of any goal you have for yourself, do you want it bad enough to do whatever it takes, within your power?

Manifesting and attracting what you want in your life is not limited to some special people. It is available to us all and we don't have to spend any money in finding out *The Secret*. Get in touch and very clear with your why. Identify a plan of action. Consistently be in a mindset of doing as well as being. Don't run away from the negative experiences. They will only stop you in your path if you allow them to. Like the *Nike* ad always says, *Just Do It.*

I hope that as you have finished reading this chapter, you have manifested your wildest dreams. If you have not, now you know what to do. Take a ride with me to a chapter that really builds upon this in *Chapter Seven: Mindfulness: It's Not Just for Breakfast Anymore.*

CHAPTER SEVEN

Mindfulness: It's Not Just for Breakfast Anymore

"No tea, no shade, no pink lemonade." - Jasmine Masters

When it comes to mindfulness, the one thing that has stuck with me for many years has been "Just for Today" from Narcotics Anonymous (NA). It goes like this, "Just for today, tell yourself: just for today my thoughts will be on my recovery, living, and enjoying life without the use of drugs. Just for today I will have faith in someone in NA who believes in me and wants to help me in my recovery. Just for today I will have a program. I will try to follow it to the best of my ability. Just for today, through NA, I will try to get a better perspective on my life. Just for today I will be unafraid. My thoughts will be on my new associations, people who are not using and who have found a new way of life. So long as I follow this way, I have nothing to fear."

This is usually read at the end of any meeting and I have to say it was a great way to close and venture out into the world. Yes, many of you reading this book are not part of a Twelve-Step program but so many philosophies in Twelve-Steps can be generalized into our daily lives and give us the tools we need to be mindful. Although they did not use the word mindfulness, their entire program rests on *just for today*. When a newcomer comes to the rooms of NA to get help, the thought of staying clean and sober for the rest of their life can be quite overwhelming. They are immediately told, and it is repeatedly reinforced, that they only have to worry about staying clean and sober today. Tomorrow, they get to make that decision again, but just for today, and only today, they can choose to remain clean and sober.

How this applies to your enlightenment is very simple. What we have been and will be discussing, along with the ongoing maintenance of what we are discussing, seems just as overwhelming as the newcomer trying to get clean and sober. Marianne Williamson says, and she takes it from the *Course*, that it is difficult not because it's hard, but because it's different. If we maintain our focus on *just for today*, this different way of being will become much less fear- and anxiety-producing.

Let's reformat the NA Just for Today for our enlightenment. Tell yourself: just for today, my thoughts will be on my enlightenment, living, and enjoying life without the control of the inner victimizer. Just for today, I will have faith in someone I love, who believes in me and wants to help me in my enlightenment. Just for today, I will be mindful. I will try to be mindful to the best of my ability. Just for today, through mindfulness, I will try to get a better perspective on my life. Just for today, I will not live in fear, anxiety, or anger. My thoughts will be on my new ways of being, people who support me and who have found a new way of life. So long as I follow this way, I have nothing to fear.

You can use just one of these lines or all of them to get you back to where you want to be.

> #ElevateNOW: Any time you step out of
> mindfulness, telling yourself "just for today"
> will snap you back to the present moment.

Let's go back to the dictionary to get clear on the word mindfulness. The dictionary defines mindfulness as 'a technique in which one focuses one's full attention only on the present, experiencing thoughts, feelings, and sensations and not judging them'. This was taken from Buddhism, which added, 'the aim is to create a state of bare awareness'.

> **#ElevateNOW: Being mindful is just being right here, right now, with no personal judgment for or against your experience.**

In previous works, I have referred to a concept called 'compassionate witness consciousness' introduced by Dr. Wayne Dyer. While I generally love his definition of the concept, it seemed too love-and-light for me. He stated, "The compassionate witness is supposed to lovingly observe all that you are experiencing, even your ego." But I think 'lovingly observe' still implies some level of judgment, albeit a good one.

> **#ElevateNow: Judgment of our experience, in general, is the one thing that kicks us out of the present moment and into the past or the future (or both).**

For instance, let's say you are having a bad day. You have judged your day as bad. The inner victimizer will now come out and start to tell you all the things in your life that are bad (probably by reminding you of something you were responsible for in your past) and how your life will continue to be bad (all future-based thinking). It's a no-brainer that negative judgment does not work towards our enlightenment. The flip side is being all love and light about things. The problem with this degree of "positive" judgment is that it bypasses and ignores any negativity, which is unrealistic. Therefore, having a sense of neutrality in our judgment creates an unbiased form of observation in which we see things more objectively and, thus, more mindfully.

It's using subjective thinking that allows judgment to occur and knocks us out of any mindfulness. Subjective thinking is all personal while objective thinking is what pretty much everyone would think about something under normal circumstances. A technique in the school of thought called Acceptance and Commitment Therapy is to project your thoughts onto a TV screen. Look at your thoughts as an observer and not as a participant. We have plenty of practice doing this, as most of us watch some sort of digital entertainment for a minimum of 30 minutes a day.

Observe the events in your life as you observe digital entertainment. Yes, we judge digital entertainment, but not until after certain stages of that entertainment has occurred. I attempted this one Saturday. I made the commitment to be in a space of nonjudgment all day. I was doing great until I got in the subway and someone asked me to simply move over so two people could sit together in the section of the train where I was sitting. There was more room on the train, but they felt it was more appropriate to ask me to move than for them to relocate to another area of the train so they could sit together. I judged it to be very entitled and immediately the inner victimizer surfaced and there went my mindfulness commitment for the rest of the day. For the record, I ended up changing seats.

There is hope in this story. Just because I failed in this attempt did not mean I threw the baby out with the bathwater. Anyone who practices meditation, which is all mindfulness, will tell you meditation is not the elimination of negative thoughts and judgment, but the non-attachment to these thoughts and judgment. In hindsight, when I saw myself falling off the wagon, I could have simply laughed it off and started over again. I elected to judge myself for failing and went on with my day judging the hell out of everything. Not the most enlightened thing I could have done, but I know better today.

#ElevateNOW: Energy flows where attention goes.

My therapist reminds me of this statement all of the time. If we give our attention over to negative thoughts and judgment, we turn our energy towards that and we are effectively knocked out of the present moment. However, if we turn our attention to the present moment, we can effectively channel our energy there. In my personal example above, when my attention turned to my failed attempt at mindfulness, I stayed in the energy of failure. However, if I had shrugged or laughed it off, and thus redirected my attention, I could have easily steered my energy back to right here, right now.

Mindfulness requires practice to make it from this woo-woo way of life to a steady state of being. It can eventually be something we do all day long as opposed to reserving it for certain times of the day or days of the week. To get to this state of being, we need to take that first step and forget about the ultimate goal for the moment. If we were to start being more mindful and then think about how hard this is going to be all day long, guess what? Your attention and energy are now diverted from being mindful.

Pick 15 minutes one day after reading this chapter. Turn your attention to those 15 minutes. You can pick a physical activity, such as eating. Maybe focus your attention on the taste of the food you are eating. Maybe count how many times you chew before you swallow. If you have a flavored beverage, how does it go with the food you are eating?

If you wanted to get really fancy about it, pick a self-care routine you really enjoy and make a commitment to yourself to be very present with it for the period of time you are doing it. These activities could easily start your mindfulness practice.

> #ElevateNOW: We can accomplish the most gigantic goals when we break them down to the smallest steps, as no step is too small.

For example, writing a book. What would be the smallest step we could take towards writing a book? Maybe it's opening up a document on your computer and typing that first sentence. Every book starts with that first sentence. You may not think this is a lot, but it is a step. Break it all down, and you will see you can accomplish any goal you set for your life.

Why is mindfulness so important? Because the present moment is the only thing we truly have. It is where everything happens. The present moment has all the power. In the present moment, we get to do everything. I think it's pretty obvious. The biggest enemies of the present are the past and the future, and our compulsive need to go back or forward that blocks the road to enlightenment.

Many schools of psychology do place a heavy emphasis on the past, sometimes too much so. Yet there comes a time when we need to leave the past behind (*Let it Go* just sprung into my head) and decide what we are going to do with all of this stuff from the past. It is unchangeable at so many levels. In the present, we get to heal our *perception* of the past, thereby creating a reverse butterfly effect. It will not change what happened, but it will change how we perceive it. This is one of the basic tenets of cognitive behavioral therapy, the school of psychology I practice. We take a look at the thoughts and behaviors that are contributing to your need for psychotherapy and devise an action plan to guide you through your enlightenment. Focusing on the past and staying in past-based events does not lead to enlightenment. That is not to say processing past traumas isn't important. I suggest to you (and to clients) to make more room for what you can do right here, right now, to bring your attention and energy to the present.

Another way we get stuck in the past is when we fear the past will repeat itself in the future. This is when we play the other 'what if' game. If you get super clear on the mistakes you made and how you contributed to them, then the focus is on building upon these lessons and being present to new ways of being. While some mistake may indeed arise in the future, I guarantee you it will not be the exact same if you stay present.

When it comes to the future, we project way too far out and come up with way too many reasons something won't work or possible disastrous outcomes. So, your attention goes in that direction. Therefore, your energy will go towards maybe *not* working for that future goal. Or maybe you'll be so cautious about every little thing you do; you actually sabotage your intended goal. Plan the plan, but don't plan the outcome. If we practice mindfulness regarding our future goals, the steps we take in the present moment will be more powerful as they will be present-focused action steps. No 'what-ifs' or 'why-mes' needed. Just who you are today and the steps you are taking right now.

> #ElevateNOW: The past is over and cannot be changed. The future has not arrived and we cannot predict it. The present controls both, through our attention and energy.

The *Course* has a line which goes, 'Hell is only what the ego has made of the present moment'. If we were to look at any one of our bad days, we will see that many of them are of our own creation and a direct result of not being mindful of our present existence. My inner victimizer's main tool is to come up with conspiracy theories. Not the Bill Gates and 5G network theory; the kind of theory that makes me think that one thing I said will cause someone to be angry with me or makes me think that when a guy doesn't return a call or a text on my timetable, he is breaking up with me. Those kind of conspiracy theories. This is where the ego/inner victimizer makes a hell in the present moment.

Another way the ego/inner victimizer makes hell in the present moment is when we incessantly ask why. Why do I keep doing this? Why do I always feel like this? Why can't I get over this? The question needn't be why. The question needs to be: what do I have to do now? Clients who work with me know that when they ask why, my response is, "The why isn't as important as the steps you need to take right here, right now. If you focus solely on the why, which is never a mindful experience, you take no action. Then, after some time, the why becomes evident. Then you take the actions you could have been taking all along."

The last thing I will share about mindfulness is a tool to get you really present really quickly, and it's something that we have conscious control over: our breath. The quickest and easiest way to get very present is focusing on our breathing. Isn't that our go-to when we are stressed out? This definitely works in a pinch; however, if you want to get really enlightened, engage in some Mindfulness-Based Stress Reduction Breathing exercises. All you do is inhale for a count of eight, hold your breath for a count of four, exhale for a count of eight and hold the out-breath for a count of four. Now, with the out breath, there is a chance you may feel some anxiety as the body may resist the lack of oxygen. Remind yourself that you are only doing it to the count of four. If that seems to be too much, change holding the out breath to the count of two. I find the counting part of it the one thing that really keeps my focus on the present moment, much like counting reps when you are weightlifting. You'll save yourself a lot of money from all of these new breathwork seminars that d*cks are hosting.

Beaming Down to Earth:

1. What mantra/affirmation could you develop for yourself to keep you in more of a *Just for Today* mentality?
2. When during the day during can practice being mindful?
3. How does your inner victimizer create hell in your present moment? How can the mindfulness tools in this chapter help you?
4. What are some self-care routines you can practice to incorporate into your mindfulness practice?

When the word mindfulness comes up, all kinds of images will pop into our heads. Yet, at its core, it's all about being in a state of awareness of your present moment as an active observer of your own experience. It has nothing to do with extended time in Tibet meditating or chugging celery juice while doing some obscure form of yoga. It is something you can do anywhere you are at any time of the day. All it takes is taking that first step and slowly building upon it.

Take a deep breath right now. Doesn't that feel good? Now that you are enlightened on being more mindful, let's take that into *Chapter Eight: Sight: More Than Meets the Eye (Yes, That One Too).*

CHAPTER EIGHT

Sight: More Than Meets the Eye (Yes, That One Too)

"If I don't understand something, I am going to smile." - Jessica Wild

Having been a comic book nerd all my life, I marveled at psychic powers. The first one to come to mind is my favorite hero of all time, Jean Grey from the *X-Men* comic books. I also loved reading the exploits of Saturn Girl in *The Legion of Superheroes* comic book. While there was a lack of male telepathic heroes as I was growing up (with the exception of Professor X from the *X-Men*), I always thought it would be so cool to read other people's minds or predict the future or move things with the power of thought.

In the late 1990s, the world was given a gift in the form of Miss Cleo. I lived for these commercials. She was a strong Black woman who laid things out for her callers. She was part of the then-popular Psychic Readers Network. I fell for one of their commercials once and, sadly, was turned off by the results. The 'psychic' would ask very leading questions and extrapolate the answers I wanted to hear. Predictions were made for future events, which is a very intelligent thing to do. It plants a seed in the caller's mind and they will subtly take actions towards that predicted event. For example, if the 'psychic' had told me I would meet my love within six months, I might have started to actively look and/or do things, such as going to singles events, to make that happen. These di*ks made a lot of money back then, yet how come we never read a headline, 'Psychic wins the lottery'? I certainly could have been happy to create that future, but this is not what we will be talking about here.

In my journey to enlightenment, I have come across many psychically gifted people. Some were clearly d*cks. However, some were pretty on the money. I would hope they would mention something only I would know or they could never know (either because they knew me or they researched my social media). I marveled at being proven wrong when I was told information there was no way they could have known about me prior to our session. I wanted to be a psychic or intuitive or what have you. I wanted to be enlightened like them. Upon more research, I discovered an amazing fact:

> #ElevateNow: We are all psychic in our own way.
> We all have intuition. We can all do this work.

What was even more mind blowing was when I realized I had this ability all along and didn't even realize it. Think about it. You meet someone and they give you bad vibes. You walk into a room and you know something is up. Someone calls you and you know something is wrong by the tone of their voice. You see something, like a commercial, on TV and you question the validity of it. These are all signs of your psychic ability. To get to a more obvious conclusion that we are all psychic, have you ever heard the term 'trust your gut'? Well, Mary, there you have it. You have had intuitive powers all along.

The term "trust your gut" relates to a psychic term called clairsentience. This is one of the four clairs, clairvoyance being the most widely known as a psychic power. They are the avenues through which we access our intuition. Notice the key term 'we'. We have access to all four clairs but some may be stronger than the other. While clairvoyance is the term most recognized, clairsentience is probably the most used by most people. The term means clear feeling. You just feel something and you can't put your finger on why. This is a psychic ability. This is your intuition at work.

This is clearly my favorite clair, especially as it pertains to the solar plexus chakra. For those of you new to chakras, they are spinning wheels of energy, almost like a spiritual nervous system. Most folks will agree we have seven (root, sacral, solar plexus, heart, throat, third eye, and crown). Each chakra is responsible for one or more source of spiritual energy. The solar plexus chakra is located in the gut and relates to your personal power and strength. Recent studies have shown the gut is more important than originally thought as it attends to the immune system, heart, brain, mood, sleep, and, of course, digestion. Many medical and healing professionals place a huge emphasis on gut health and there are many resources you can access for that. However, knowing the stomach is that important and powerful, we would do well to take care of it to improve our psychic abilities. If our gut is that important and related to clairsentience, we would do well to pay more attention to it.

Clairvoyance is not just what we hear about it in the media. It refers to clear seeing. While some people actually do see stuff (and not in a hallucinatory way), many of us will have clear seeing that looks a lot different when we get street-level enlightened. On a psychological level, studies have shown that eyewitnesses can see vastly differently things about the same event. On an individual scale, you probably see many things differently than other people in your life see them. This sight is influenced by not only your likes and dislikes, but also by past experiences.

Clairvoyance can simply be looking at things in a different way. Suspend disbelief and look through your other sight, not just your physical vision. We all have visions about our life and life in general. They can be so crystal clear for us. Some folks would also say that if you see things repeatedly, like a certain set of numbers or maybe butterflies, this is also a form of clairvoyance. Taking note of all of these things and being mindful of this vision is your form of clairvoyance.

Clear thinking is claircognizance. This is probably one of the least common clairs in my personal research, yet it's something most of us do all of the time. It refers to clear thinking. Ever hear of 'thinking outside the box'? There is your claircognizance. Something popped into your mind, and there it goes again. All of these forms of thinking are related to your claircognizance. There was a character in one of the *X-Factor* series. Her name was Layla Miller and her catchphrase was, "I know stuff." This irked her teammates a great deal, but certainly she was a valuable member of the team. We all know stuff, yet this form of knowing goes way beyond the intellectual.

Another way our claircognizance takes form in our lives is through of aha moments. The reason why these aha moments are so powerful is because we are in that full state of knowing. When we have an aha moment, it's not something that we just feel meh about. It's literally a moment in which we feel inspired and energized. This is the level beyond the intellectual.

And lastly, you have clairaudience, which is clear hearing. When you listen to a song, what do you hear? It's not just the lyrics, but how it speaks to you at a whole different level than just what the artist sang. You are hearing at a deeper level. Another example (which has happened to me so many times) is when you know you have heard something a million times but it took that one right way to be said for you to hear it. Add to this that the information you just heard that right time you heard exactly when you needed it to.

While some folks with psychic abilities actually hear things (again, not in a hallucinatory way), you may want to pay attention to them if you do as well. While many aha moments are more in the claircognizance realm, we can also achieve aha moments with our clairaudient abilities. It's the moment when we hear something out of nowhere.

The truth is, we really all can be psychic. We all have these abilities. We have all used our intuition at some point in our lives. While some individuals have a higher sensitivity or ability to use them, that does not negate the fact that we all have these abilities to some degree or another.

> **#ElevateNOW: You can develop any one (or all) of your clairs, actively seeking to look beyond the superficial. You can have more than one, and even all four, clairs.**

I will be honest, the use of the word clairs makes me nuts as it makes something we all have into something so woo-woo. Go ahead and call it whatever you like. One way to develop your clairs is to look beyond what you see.

I will elaborate. My friends goof on me because I see the higher consciousness meaning behind most anything I see or read, even when it's not the intention. However, being able to 'see' more than what is there with your physical senses is a surefire way of becoming more in tune with your psychic abilities and intuition.

An amazing example of this is a character on one of my favorite TV shows, *DC's Legends of Tomorrow*. The main character, Sarah Lance, aka The White Canary, was a bit of a spoiled socialite until she was in a boating accident and presumed dead. She was found by the League of Assassins and trained to be one of them. She returned to her home city and faced her loved ones. She rejected her League training and became the superhero The Black Canary. She was subsequently killed by the League, resurrected by her ex-lover (Oliver Queen) and her sister (who assumed the mantle of the Black Canary in her "absence"), and became a hero in her own right, leading a team of ragtag heroes and villains to rights wrongs across history while battling the inner demons of her assassin past.

What prompted me to include this in the chapter on psychic abilities is how her storyline has inspired me to develop my own inner White Canary. I knew her journey because my inner victimizer likes to remind me of my past with my own League of Assassins. I, too, have thought to myself, who am I to lead and be forgiven for my past? I heard her words of encouragement to her team and loved ones. I felt her journey from darkness into the light. I didn't just see the show—I felt it on all levels of my being, and this is a very simple way to develop your psychic ability. Go beyond what you see with your physical senses.

If all else fails, we may want to pay attention to something. Think back to a major decision in your life. Did you hear two voices? I know I always do. One voice speaks in a normal tone and volume. It speaks to me like I would speak to a client in a therapy session. Then there is the voice of the inner victimizer. This voice is super loud, maybe to the point of screaming. This voice wants us to take the first course of action that will lead to immediate gratification. It wants us to rush into or out of a decision. The other, quieter voice simply states what a course of action could be. This softer voice is your intuition. This is your psychic ability. Learn to listen to this voice, even though the inner victimizer will speak first and it will speak the loudest.

As you can see, the way psychic abilities are explained in comic books and sci-fi looks quite different than mind powers in real life. What the inner victimizer will tell you about other people's thoughts is not trustworthy information. This is not intuition. This is the inner victimizer's way of furthering the narrative that you are not as good as others and you couldn't possibly be as enlightened as them.

Here are some simple tricks to use our psychic abilities more often. It will require a greater degree of mindfulness than we may be used to; however, we went over that already and you now know you are all mindfulness gurus. When your gut is telling you something, trust that. If you're struggling too much with something, you may want to rethink it. If you are hearing something a certain way, pay attention to that. It's that simple. No tarot cards or crystal balls needed—unless you want them.

Beaming Down to Earth:

1. What are your fears and/or concerns about psychic abilities? Identify the source(s) and rework that script.
2. Using what has been discussed in this chapter, which one (or more) of the four clairs do you think you most closely identify with?
3. Which one of the four clairs would you like to develop into a stronger ability? Using what was discussed in this chapter, how will you go about doing so?
4. Think about some of your favorite songs, movies, books, and TV shows. What is it about these that appeals to you and makes you feel more alive? That's your psychic ability at work.

Being psychic is nothing more than being in touch with your higher senses. We all have the ability to some degree or another. You don't have to join the Psychic Readers Network or even read tarot cards if you don't want to. You need to get in touch with those things that go beyond your physical senses, as the word psychic is defined. You can have clear seeing, clear feeling, clear hearing, and/or clear thinking if you allow yourself to. Give yourself the permission to get to know the world and yourself in a different light.

Let's jump ahead into something that has become almost as necessary as our dominant arm: social media. We can use social media to be more enlightened but we have to do so in such a way as to not be di*ks. Flip the page to *Chapter Nine, Social Media and Technology: Do These Calvins Make Me Look Fat?*

CHAPTER NINE

Social Media and Technology: Do These Calvins Make Me Look Fat?

"You are shadier than a palm tree." - April Carrion

Social media has become one of the most important things in our lives. During the coronavirus pandemic and subsequent quarantines, one of the ways we stayed in touch and connected with others was with social media. Yet, social media can breed so much inauthenticity that it makes one crazy. There are so many d*cks on social media. Many days, the authenticity on social media is probably 25% of the posts you see. The use of social media has caused many arguments between loved ones. It has destroyed relationships, companies, and careers. While some of these collapses were well deserved, others may not have been. To be truly Enlightened as Hell, we need to have a mindset in our use of social media that is reflective of our enlightened state. Fortunately, we already have the tools from the preceding chapters to show up on social media as authentic as you are—and not just as you have the potential to be.

When you have done the work from Chapter One, you will have some sense of what your inner champion is. As fluid as this can be across a lifespan, at the moment you fire up any of the social media apps, you get in touch right away with that part of you. This accomplishes two things: you know who you are at that moment, and you can set an active intention about it. Think back to your last few posts on any of the social media platforms.

Can you say you posted all of them from that space of authenticity, your inner champion?

> **#ElevateNOW: The key to being Enlightened**
> **as Hell on social media is making sure your**
> **posts reflect your inner champion and not**
> **just the self you want others to see.**

Do not curate what you post with the intention of giving people what they want to see so you can get the likes and stuff. Give them who you *are* in your posts. Enlightenment entails people seeing who you are. This comes with a lot of the work from Chapter 1. When I am feeling a certain way, I do not hide it from my social media. I get very raw about whatever is going on. The way I structure these posts is by being raw about the issue as well as being raw with the solution, whether it's a solution I like or don't. The key is being raw and not emotionally vomiting.

Emotional vomiting on social media is not engaging with your inner champion. Many times, people who do so are seeking something such as attention, validation, or sympathy. Sometimes I have seen folks actually try to get people to agree with them so they can be convinced that whatever they are spewing is correct and true. This is not being raw. This is not reflective of your inner champion. This is not Enlightened as Hell.

If we are coming from our inner champion in our posts, we wouldn't need validation, sympathy, or attention. A raw post could look something like this: 'Doubt—ever have one of those days when everything you think about, you downplay because you are doubting yourself? Welcome to my world today. My inner saboteur is striking down everything faster than I can plan things out. Sometimes the secret is just doing the action despite the inner saboteur's screams. Physically do something towards what you want (write it down, make a post) because that allows for some lessening of the voice of the IS (that b*tch). Literally just do it'. To show you the contrast, an emotionally vomiting post can look like this: 'Ugh, like FML. Sephora ran out of the foundation I really love and they won't be getting it back for a while. What should I do? I just won't look right without it'.

Our inner champion knows what's true for us. It does not need anything external. Therefore, if you set your intention as such, you will come across as very enlightened.

Sadly, one thing that social media can breed is comparison. The inner victimizer will take a look at someone else's post(s) and start to speak up. It wants to convince you that this other person is better than you and you will never measure up to them. Here is where you grab the tools and say to yourself, "This person is not better than me and I am not better than them." Remind yourself of your strengths and what you want to authentically share in your posts. Actively steer away from what they may have that you don't. Share that one strength you identified earlier in this book and run with it. You will be surprised at the response you will receive.

#ElevateNOW: By staying in touch with our inner champion, we focus less on validation and comparison while showing the world of social media how enlightened we are.

While positive feedback is nice and helpful, our inner champion does not need validation from the social media world. To be enlightened on social media, we would do best to focus on showing our authentic selves, flaws and all, instead of obsessing over the need to look good and post what will get the most likes.

This question has saved my butt so any times on social media. When that fear, or even the active choice to not love, sets in, our human response is to lash out to feel a sense of power. There are so many things to be angry about on social media. We can literally see the worst of humanity. Do we want to join in with that?

We need to be very mindful of how we respond to haters and trolls on social media if we want to be Enlightened as Hell. The reality is that no matter how raw and authentic and vulnerable you are on social media, no matter how long you take in preparing your post to secure your intention, there will always be someone to find fault in it. The key is to remember it is not about you and all about them. My simple way to respond to haters and trolls on social media is simple: 'Thank you for sharing, have a nice day'. It acknowledges their presence and shuts down any further conversation. It is a response based in love, not in agreement or disagreement with what the other person is saying.

The *Course* teaches, 'We create what we defend against'. If I decide to engage with a hater on social media to defend my stance, I will likely end up creating more of what I don't want. By being defensive with another (in general, not just on social media), you create more defensiveness in the other person. They believe they are right and you believe you are right.

#ElevateNOW: When you know you are right
and stand in that power, you don't have to prove
another person wrong. You can coexist.

86

Getting revenge on a hater/troll on social media does not exemplify 'only love is real'. You are the one doing the work to be enlightened and trying to show that on your social profiles. Your inner champion cannot be harmed; therefore, why do you need to lash out at the haters? Furthermore, if we are in touch with our inner champion, why do we spend so much time worrying about how others will perceive us online? Standing in the truth of who we are and showing this to the world is the most enlightened thing we can do.

Social media can be very fertile soil to strengthen our concept of our inner champion. Whether we are being vulnerable or curating our posts to generate likes, we still open ourselves up for disapproval. I would rather be disapproved of for being me than for being fake. This will be your main tool in working through your fear of being authentic on social media.

If you do have a hater or if someone judged you negatively for your content, let's look back at objective and subjective fears. Is what they are saying negatively about you something that will compromise your physical well-being? Most likely not, unless they actually make a threat of physical violence (in these cases, contact your local authorities, because doing so is very enlightened). What is being injured is our perception of what should be happening (subjective fear), that everyone needs to love and agree with us on social media all the time. Reality says this is not the case, as there will always be people who disagree with us. This is an uncomfortable yet liberating truth. Do you want to be a victim of digital hate or a champion of your own enlightenment?

Forgiving our haters is easy if we apply Jack Kornfield's definition of forgiveness. We can simply and objectively state that something has gone wrong. The turning point for us enlightened folks is to not make this wrongness about us. While we would do well to objectively listen to constructive feedback, we don't need to internalize hate and add more food to the inner victimizer's already full refrigerator. Once we have identified what truly and objectively went wrong, we can then make the active choice to not allow it to affect our continued enlightened presence on social media. This is how 'forgive and delete' works on social media.

> **#ElevateNOW: When facing hate on social media, we would be enlightened to remember that this is not about us; this is how they respond to the world.**

So many haters are very negative on their own profiles. The only bad review for my first book was by someone who literally gave a bad review to nine out of 10 books they read. This is who they are, unfortunately. Nothing I can do to directly change that. Here we bring in what Elsa reminds us of, and we choose to let it go. It's difficult only because it is so different from what we are used to doing. If we can't change something, why hold on to it? This only feeds the inner victimizer's need to control everything around us and keep us miserable. Feel your feelings but do what you need to do for yourself, regardless of the hate.

We can never control the actions of other people on social media. We only control how we choose to respond to it. If you choose to respond, what would be your motives in doing so? Is it to prove yourself right or are you intending to attempt a meaningful dialogue with them? If we can't come from a place of love, forgiveness, and surrender, it would be more enlightened of us to not respond at all. This practice is not weakness, but strength and enlightenment on our part.

> **#ElevateNOW: Always, always, always check your motives for posting something.**

To be Enlightened as Hell on social media, we have to be in touch with whatever is the true motive for what we are posting. If your motives are not in alignment with your enlightened state, be prepared to get the response you get. I have seen where I have made posts that were in alignment with my path to enlightenment; however, opinions are like anuses and everyone has one. Creating posts that are in alignment with our inner champion does not guarantee an absence of negativity or haters. However, our need to defend ourselves, as well as our fears, can diminish greatly.

> **#ElevateNOW: Being enlightened on social media is less about what you need to do and more of who you need to be.**

We can use the tricks in the *Law of Distraction* chapter perfectly on social media. We just discussed the need to be in touch with our motives, which will place us in the mindset and behavioral pattern to create what we want. This will be reflected in the content of our posts. You see it all the time, even with the d*cks whose motives are quite selfish.

Think of all the times you fell for something you saw on social media. Think back to what you were drawn to. Usually, what hooked you was the promise of something better. Here, you may have forgotten about your inner champion and allowed the inner victimizer to come in and tell you that you needed this. You went for it. After completion of whatever it was that you fell for, you sit in misery that you did not get the results you wanted. Yet the d*ck on social media who sold you on it has your money. This was their motive. Change this around to make it work for you to share your enlightenment with the world.

> **#ElevateNow: The enlightened thought is not 'what if' but 'what do I want now?'**

Whenever we engage in any behavior, the inner victimizer likes to remind us, 'Well, what if this doesn't work?' The fear of being vulnerable, raw, and authentic is very scary, even more so on social media as you may have a ton of followers. The fear-based question of 'what if' will creep up. If you have not been paying attention, nothing in this path (and in the world in general) can guarantee you results. If we stick to who we are and not who we want people to see, the people who matter will take notice.

> **#ElevateNOW: When being attacked on social media, we can look/see/hear/think beyond the venom and remain in our enlightened state.**

This is also the time to use your psychic abilities to deal with haters. All we would need to do is look beyond the hate. When anyone attacks from a place of hate, many times you find a very wounded person. Attacking with hate is usually an attempt to grasp at power and control. This is what you will always find lies beyond the venom. Additionally, a lot of constructive feedback can be found in the hate we receive. We are invincible but not infallible. Add humility to your psychic abilities and see where you can do things differently.

Another way to use your psychic powers is to touch base with yourself before you post. Does this post feel right? Can I hear the message I am trying to send? Does this post accurately reflect what I was thinking when I wrote it? Am I seeing my intention in this post? Get real with yourself and your posts with your psychic abilities.

Share your thoughts, and don't shame others because they don't think the same way you do. Sure, being shady may be called for from time to time, but you don't want to be shady all the time. Speaking our enlightened truth(s) carries enough power to counteract whatever falsities are being shared on social media. Whether you have one follower or one million, you have a platform. Use it for your enlightenment and the enlightenment of others.

Beaming Down to Earth:

1. What are you biggest fears associated with being your real, raw, and authentic self on social media?
2. What are your biggest fears about criticism from readers on social media?
3. Since judgment may be the answer to the first two questions, why aren't you being in the space of your inner champion?
4. Do a first draft for a post on your social media that is super raw and vulnerable. Read it over. Sit with it. Now, post it.

Being enlightened on social media is not difficult, but it is different. It calls to action a sense of self-awareness and intentionality we may not be used to practicing. It has everything to do with us and virtually nothing to do with your following. Of course, you want to have messages your readers will resonate with; however, it needs to resonate with you first. Worrying about the haters and acting like a d*ck does not lead us down towards a path of enlightenment. On the contrary, it gives the inner victimizer more fuel to go off. Be your own champion and not the victim of subjective fear.

It's great to follow a discussion about social media with a discussion on spirituality and making money. Onwards now to *Chapter 10: Making Money: Pimping Ain't Easy.*

CHAPTER TEN

Making Money: Pimping Ain't Easy

"Manual labor is not my thing." - Naomi Smalls

Making money and being enlightened appear to be mutually exclusive. Some religions have their ordained people take a vow of poverty and renounce all personal property. Buddhist monks, priests, and nuns renounced Earthly pleasures. In the Bible, Matthew says, 'No one can serve two masters. Either he will hate the one and love the other, or he will be devoted to one and despise the other. You cannot serve both God and money'.

The Book of Proverbs says, 'Dishonest money dwindles away, but whoever gathers money little by little makes it grow'. Between cultural themes involving money and what various religious schools of thought teach, it's almost like making money is associated with the Devil, or evil, or greed. This may be the underpinnings of an unhealthy relationship with money for a lot of us. Yet making money can be an essential part of our enlightenment if we know how to go about it.

> #ElevateNOW: Making money is an essential part of your enlightenment because it forces you to take a look at yourself, your abilities, and your motives to such a degree that you push your journey that much more forward.

Here is where I am coming from regarding the subject matter. I have seen so many d*cks manipulate people into buying stuff (courses, products, etc.) even when the person really can't afford it. The seller will say something along the lines of, "Well, if you can't take a stand for your own transformation, who will?" Some will go so far as to suggest a second mortgage or taking out a loan to purchase said stuff. On the flip side, I have seen way too many d*cks sell courses and stuff they have no business selling, either by virtue of lack of training and/or experience. Many other d*cks exploit current events to make money. There is nothing enlightened about any of these methods.

For this chapter, I consulted with various individuals from all walks of life who run a successful spiritually based or successful spiritually adjacent business to get their real-world feedback on the subject matter. Since money is such a hot-button issue and this is a book on street-level everyday enlightenment, I thought it best to give you various real-world viewpoints. The themes covered are balancing making money while being spiritual and ethical, the spiritual keys to financial success, measuring success, thoughts on passive income, and the trendy notion of working less but earning more.

Anyone who has ever been employed in sales or in the service industry knows how hard it is to balance making money with being spiritual and ethical. In a past life, I worked as a bartender. I know how much kissing up to customers weighed heavily on the tip received. When I was working as an administrator in several mental health programs, keeping referral sources happy was one of my main duties. The struggle for me was always how to maintain a balance between keeping that cash flowing and being spiritual and ethical about it.

> #ElevateNow: Making money and being
> enlightened all boils down to one thing:
> your intentions for doing either.

My first thought on the matter goes back to a theme we have discussed many times so far, which is intention. What is my intention in engaging in this action to make money? Is it solely to make money or does it serve a greater purpose? In my line of work, there are many venues that are very lucrative. On the surface, they are also quite ethical. However, the main reason why I won't engage in these lines of business is because I don't like how I feel after I am done. While the revenue stream is nice and affords me certain luxuries, the price is way too much for me to pay. It's like these revenue streams suck all the light out of my enlightenment.

Michael Anthony, spiritual life coach at The Diviner Life, says his balance between making money and being spiritual and ethical comes from the question, 'Am I putting people first? I ask if those people are my priority or if the money is. If money is ever the priority, I start over'.

Theresa Reed, aka The Tarot Lady, says, "My focus is rooted squarely in service. When your intention is there instead of worrying about numbers, your decisions will always come from a place of integrity. I also never take on work that feels out of alignment with my ethics. If it feels off, I have no problem saying no, even if it affects my bottom line."

Yet when it comes to money and spirituality and enlightenment, I have come across folks who have issues with asking for what they are worth. Jonathan Hammond, shamanic practitioner and spiritual counselor at Mind Body Spirit NYC and author of *The Shaman's Mind*, says, "Money exchange is part of the healing. Without the investment, the clients take less responsibility." He adds, "Being mindful to charge what I am worth but not to go overboard. Rock star prices imply rock star expectations (of myself and others). Very dicey."

The common thread in the responses provided by these practitioners are firmly rooted in the practices of integrity, putting people first and charging according to who you are. As noted in Hammond's response, asking for money is part of the relationship with his clients and the relationship between his clients and their respective healing. The intention you put into fees becomes grounded in intentionality and not in the actual amount.

> **#ElevateNOW: The spiritual keys to financial success have nothing to do with money at all.**

So, with all this being said, what are some spiritual keys to financial success? I keep it very simple for myself: do I feel good at the end of the day with the services I provided and the money I charged for those services? Does what I do for others not only serve as a key to their enlightenment but my own as well? In my practice, I accept private and government-funded insurances. The fees they pay their providers are much lower than for peers who charge fees and don't take insurance. The reason I feel good about this is it makes me more accessible to most individuals who can't afford to pay out of pocket for therapy. I am not throwing any shade at my colleagues at all. This is the choice I made when I opened my business because it was in alignment with who I want to be in the world.

Damon L. Jacobs, licensed marriage and family therapist in New York City, measures success as follows: "Begin from God; money will come. It's kind of a cliché but it's really true for me. When I have approached job interviews, opportunities, therapy work, and speaking gigs from a position of loving God energy, then quite often they have resulted in making more money."

Jacobs adds, "Do good work. If you're going to do a job, if you're going to make money, then do it with integrity, with kindness." I particularly enjoyed Jacobs's statement of: "Treat people with respect. Treat them like vehicles of God they are. That means treating EVERYONE at the agency with kindness and respect, not just the people directly paying you."

Jill Drader, workshop facilitator and consultant, feels her keys to spiritual success are found in alignment. She says, "Aligning with calling and attracting what you need, not this bullsh*t six-figures and work a b*tch out. It's not about taking everyone on. It's about taking the right people in."

The spiritual keys to success begin with what I previously said: focus more on who you need to be and less on what you need to do. It begins with us and who we want to be in the money-generating actions we choose to undertake. This looks different from person to person. My preference is in speaking to a live audience, for instance, as opposed to filming a webinar for sale. Now, if the webinar topic is something I feel is in alignment with who I want to be, then I have to work through my personal issues with being on camera (all the inner victimizer's doing, by the way).

> #ElevateNOW: Measuring your success has nothing to do with numbers. It has everything to do with being and doing.

Measuring success can be not only difficult, but very subjective. Yet, if we choose to redefine what the word success means for us, we will be better able to measure it. In my work with clients, success for me is measured in the change I am able to facilitate for them and the client's ability to translate this change into their daily lives. With my writing career, I will be very honest and admit I have made very little money as a writer. However, readers have contacted me from across the globe, sharing with me how the words in my books have changed their lives for the better. In both instances, the way I measure success is in how I am able to facilitate change for others.

Unbeknownst to me at the outset, the business people I consulted had very similar answers. Michael Anthony measures success as follows: "Success to me is measured one person at a time. Every time my work—in some way—reminds a person that life is worth living, I know I am successful."

Theresa Reed shares a similar philosophy: ". . . by the results I get for people. When a client comes back and tells me that the reading helped them, I know I have done my job. Happy feedback from people who found my work to be helpful is the true measure of success."

Jacobs's philosophy is also very similar. He says, "If I can end the day feeling like I did God's work the best I could, that is a success. If I feel like I raised someone's mood or mind, perhaps gave them a different way to see a problem, a new thought system that provides a conduit to feeling joy and pleasure, then that is a success."

Hammond takes a more personal approach to measuring success. "By taking responsibility. I take note of the quality of what goes on between my ears at any given moment. Cleaning up stuff, at least enough that my stuff doesn't spill over into another's experience."

The measurement of success, according to everyone involved in this chapter, has little, if anything, to do with money. It is all about the place we need to be within ourselves and how our work impacts others. Bank accounts and social media follows don't have much to do with true success.

#ElevateNOW: There is nothing passive about passive income. It always involves some level of work.

I have seen a shift towards venues that generate passive income. Personally, I never have found this to be energetically pleasurable nor does it feel very enlightened at all. However, I know my opinion on the matter is biased based on my upbringing and, quite frankly, I just love to work and be in contact with people all the time. Passive sources of income, while potentially lucrative, eliminate the opportunities for that one-on-one connection with others. My father also taught us the value of working hard for what you have because you appreciate it more. Therefore, I find passive income streams to have little value to me beyond money.

With regard to passive income, Michael Anthony has this to say: "Passive should not mean disconnected. If you generate passive income in the spiritual world, you'd better be sure you're still active and engaged with the lives affected." Jonathan Hammond is of a similar mindset. He says, "It's great. For me, it means producing worthwhile products and that takes time."

Theresa Reed and I seem to be on the same page. She says, "Passive income is a myth. It's not really passive. You still have to market the hell out of it."

Jill Drader provided the following similar point of view: "Passive income is a myth, I think. If you want to be passive in your life or in your business, be passive. On the 'how you do one thing is how you do everything' model: this isn't great alignment for value."

In addition, affiliate marketing, a passive stream of income, seems good in theory but the reality is you need to hustle in affiliate marketing. You have to reach out to people consistently, make social media posts about the thing you are marketing (generating large amounts of money for someone else while you get some scraps), and sadly, sell your soul to really make a go at it. Selling your soul definitely does not lead to enlightenment.

Here are the bottom lines on affiliate marketing that you need to remember: you need to find the right one. The market is pretty flooded with affiliate marketing venues. You advertise the product or service and while that generates money for the producer, it doesn't always translate into cash for you. If you are going to do affiliate marketing, do it with a product and/or service you love.

Passive income does not mean you sit on your couch and watch money just come in. It requires a bit more of internal work as well as actual physical labor. It's not about earning money the easy way. It's about earning money and being real about yourself and accountable to the people you may impact.

> **#ElevateNow: Easy money does not translate into better. It's just easy.**

Also, I stumbled across a book one time that had the title *The Four-Hour Work Week* and it bothered me to no end. When did working hard become such a bad thing? I feel we are strongly influenced by the immediate gratification of today's world. Yet that shifted during coronavirus quarantine. We had some ability to get our needs met and goods delivered, but a good majority missed the opportunity to do just about anything for ourselves.

Michael Anthony believes in "working smarter and earning your accumulated value. At some point, the work gets easier and therefore can be perceived as less effort, but should never actually be less value." Along these same lines, Damon Jacobs feels "no matter the quantity of time I put in, I just hope the quality is valuable for the people I serve".

Theresa Reed says, "If someone wants to make a lot of money without doing the work, that's up to them. It's just not how I roll. I'd rather be doing something." Jonathan Hammond shares a similar belief as Reed, saying, "Sounds good, but this sounds like new-agey-secret-formula-that-only-I-know-so-take-my-class. Working less and earning more comes from the quality of one's work".

Jill Drader provides a more contrasting point of view. She says, "We are coming out of a theme of capitalistic drive that isn't working for everyone. Less work for others is more time to serve and reflect and be, create more loving and solid communities. I think we need that".

I think the general consensus here is to work smarter and not harder. While this could lead to a four-hour work week, do you really want that?

Some final thoughts on being enlightened and making money: make a career for yourself and earn a decent income without ripping people off. It is very possible. The more you throw your enlightenment into who you are, the more it will attract the customers you want. And if you want to be truly enlightened, never manipulate your consumers or prey on their weaknesses. That's plain trashy.

Beaming Down to Earth:

1. Take a look at your relationship with making money. How has that defined you in the past? How would you like it to define you moving forward?
2. When in your money-making mentality, who do you become? Do you like this person? Do others like this person?
3. If you were at the place where you were generating enough income to work less, what would you be doing with your spare time and how would that make the world a better place?
4. Your consumers are spending money on you and/or your services. Are you very clear on who and what this is before collecting any money?

This was a pretty intense chapter, but one that needed to be included. Making money is an essential part of your enlightenment because it forces you to be very intentional as to who you are and how you are impacting others in your quest to earn some good coin. Don't be scared of making money in your path towards enlightenment, but don't let making money turn you away from your enlightenment.

Whether your wallet is heavy with all the money you made or you are broke as hell, let's take a stroll into how all of this looks like on a day-to-day basis in *Chapter 11: Practices: Meditate and Then Go Have Sex With Your Partner(s)*.

CHAPTER ELEVEN

Practices: Meditate and Then Go Have Sex With Your Partner(s)

"My name is Adore Delano and I'm a messy slut." - Adore Delano

When I took my Reiki training (a form of energy healing), the symbols and the order in which we were taught to do things to practice Reiki out in the real world were quite daunting. My physical coordination isn't great and that translates into one hot uncoordinated mess. Yet one thing my instructors said that stuck with me and has allowed me to practice some form of Reiki was, 'Reiki works by intention'. The word intention has been used quite a bit throughout this book as it's really the cornerstone of your enlightenment. We may not know all the religious dogmas and deities, we may not have all the moves down to perform some sort of ritual or healing rite, but we do have control over walking into any spiritual practice with intention.

> #ElevateNOW: Just about anything is a spiritual practice as long as you have the intention behind it.

So many spiritual practices rely on the user's intention to fortify whatever ritual you are working on. Write your intention on a piece of paper and then . . . say this prayer or affirmation with the intention of . . . or any combination of both. Anything that requires the user stating their intention out loud and affirming it to themselves (and perhaps others). The Buddhists speak heavily on karma, which is loosely defined as 'actions defined by intention'. If so many organized religions and spiritual schools of thought rely on or focus on intention, so can we in our path towards enlightenment.

Intention is defined as 'purpose or attitude towards the effects of one's actions or conduct'. This means walking into something with a specific direction in your mind. The reason this chapter is one of the last is because we needed to walk through all the previous steps to get to a point where we know ourselves better and have some idea in mind for our lives. Yet in this very human world full of immediate gratification, we have competing priorities and/or desires. We have fears. We recover from trauma. The global landscape changed so drastically with coronavirus. Anything can distract us from our intention and it does. The key is to get back on track as soon as you notice yourself getting off track.

One way to keep yourself in your intention is to ask yourself one question. I refer to one of my favorite books written for gay men, *The Velvet Rage* by Dr. Alan Downs. While the first two-thirds of the book is pretty much written for gay men, the last third of the book speaks about skills for living an authentic life. The first skill Dr. Downs refers to is, "What would the man I wish to become do in this situation?" This question has had the most profound impact in my life, not only as a gay man but in my path to enlightenment and in the practices I use in my daily life to continue to work towards my enlightenment.

If you have not done so, I want you to get in touch with the most ideal sense of self you possibly can for a moment. You can visualize it or even write it down. Keep this sense of self accessible to you. If you are having trouble with that, I would have you use The Miracle Questions, which is quite popular in psychotherapy and which I have used many times with clients: "If you woke up tomorrow morning and this problem was gone, what would your life look like? How would you know this problem had been solved?"

In psychotherapy, this allows for the client to picture a life without their issues defining them. It liberates them from whatever has been imposed on them (either by others or themselves) and gives them a goal to strive for. You can use a modified version of The Miracle Questions to get to an ideal sense of self by simply asking, "The person I wish to become, what do they look like? How do they see the world? How do they carry themselves in this world? How do they interact with others in this world?" Write these answers down and keep them handy.

Keep in mind that this sense of self will change and mutate over time. When I originally read *The Velvet Rage* around 2010, my ideal self looked different than the vision I have for myself today. That is absolutely fine, as this allows for continued growth and enlightenment.

When you are confronted with a situation, ask yourself the question, "What would the person I wish to become do in this situation?" This is the easiest way to zap you back into the present moment and into your intention. So, when it comes time for you to develop the practices you want to continually engage in to get you and keep you on your path to enlightenment, get very clear on your intention. This intention can be fairly easy to determine once you get clear on some sense of what your ideal self looks like. What are you intending by engaging in this practice? And here's a major bonus point: this question is just as pertinent in any area of your life as well.

#ElevateNOW: The person you wish to become is enlightened. It is also all about your inner champion.

105

You don't have to go very far to get to a sense of ideal self or your intention. It's already there. Much like *A Course in Miracles* says about 'removing the blocks to the awareness of love's presence', our spiritual practices will allow us to remove the obstacles to the awareness of our inner champion. If we make it a habit to silence the inner victimizer, and to reach within and get in touch with our inner champion, half the journey is complete.

One of the biggest problems, if not the biggest problem, in most religions and current pop culture spirituality movements is that things have to look a certain way for something to be spiritual. There is an inherent problem in telling another person what their path needs to look like when you are not walking their path. One of the biggest struggles I have ever had in my enlightenment has been reconciling sex and spirituality. The kicker is that the struggles were created by the priests, nuns, and brothers in the Catholic Church, who had taken a vow of celibacy. Why I never questioned that is beyond me.

Sex was always demonized in the Catholic Church, gay sex, even more so. Gay men in general are never taught to have a healthy relationship with sex. Even when I was in the closet and was dating women, I don't know if I ever had a healthy relationship with sex. If you have paid any attention to the various topics the inner victimizer loves to torture us with, sex is definitely one of the top five. Sex was probably one of the hardest lessons in my path to enlightenment.

> **#ElevateNOW: Sex is a spiritual practice
> in your enlightenment if you approach
> it with the proper intention.**

My psychotherapy practice primarily focuses on serving the LGBT community. The majority of my clients are gay men. It's almost ingrained in us that our worth comes from sex. We are expected to be promiscuous and therefore live up to that standard . . . or try to. But for many of us, this does not always feel right. The question I pose to them is always, "Do you want to have sex to get some sort of validation or do you have a true desire from sex independent of validation?" This is where we transform the act of casual sex into a spiritual experience.

Let's look at the difference (and many of us have been in this situation, regardless of sexual orientation). During lower points, and certainly not my most enlightened times, I engaged in sex for the purposes of numbing and/or validating. The result was also the same. Sometimes I had a great time, but all the pain kept coming back. Other times, I did not have a great time and felt even worse than I did before. I wouldn't focus on connecting with another human being as my intention was that they were a means to an end. I reduced sex to a transaction. But there have been several occasions in which I have engaged in sex with someone I connected with, someone I got to know beforehand, someone with whom I wanted to be connected, and not with any physical appendages per se. In those instances, sex became a spiritual practice and part of my path towards enlightenment.

When I approach sex with the intention of connecting with someone else AND being my most authentic self, I learn more about me than I do in any other spiritual activity. In those moments, I intentionally allow myself to get to know another person in probably the most intimate way. I also get to know myself in a more intimate way. I remove any obstacles and am fully immersed in the moment. How is this not enlightened behavior?

For some extra sexual enlightenment, I reached out to my friend Amy Jindra, who is a tantra coach. She says the following about sex as a spiritual practice, "Approaching sex as advancing you forward by giving you the knowledge of who you are in those moments". She further says, "You can bring a meditative practice to sex. This could involve breathing, your energetic fields, patience, and compassion to slow down your brain and really be present with your partner. You find these moments of 'in between,' where you don't have a personality or a childhood with a past or future. You only have what you are in these moments and that's when you grow exponentially. It's based on who you are and what you feel without all the conditioning, even in the moments of orgasm".

> #ElevateNow: There are so many different practices you can engage in towards your enlightenment that you won't have to worry about picking the wrong one. The wrong ones will show themselves out.

So, this chapter is about practices, and I have not mentioned any real practices yet. There's a reason for that. I can rattle off a list of 100 different things you can do. However, the one thing I will tell you is that you need to find the one(s) that work for you and the only way to know that is to pick one or more and try them on for yourself.

If you are new to this work or maybe have fallen off the wagon in your enlightenment, my rule of thumb is to keep it super simple. We may have heard of folks who meditate for 20 minutes twice a day or go on weeklong silent retreats and things like that. Yet the simplest act can do just as much as a weekend yoga retreat.

My personal practice, at minimum, is as follows: I wake up early most days and drink some room-temperature water with freshly squeezed lemon—I don't know why I do but it seems to work. I stay away from social media. I go to a section of my bedroom and sit in a designated space on a meditation cushion. I use singing bowls briefly to set the mood. Sometimes, I will incorporate incense. Usually, I will pull a tarot card and think about its meaning in my personal life. I spend a minimum of three minutes simply focusing on my breath. I make sure to take deep breaths in and deep breaths out. Sometimes I envision my inner champion and maybe bring in other spiritual deities I believe in. Once I come out of the breathing, I will read a page or two from a thought-for-the-day type book and I am done. This particular practice is literally a hodgepodge of practices that have now come together to make my daily routine at the present time. I have not perfected a method for staying enlightened throughout the day, but definitely have the things that work for me.

The best practice you can engage in is meditation. While this word strikes fear in some, it is really quite simple in execution. I have heard folks say, "Oh, I can't quiet my mind down enough to meditate" or "I don't have the time to meditate." Meditation is as simple as focusing on your breath. Go back to Chapter Seven and practice the Mindfulness-Based Stress Reduction Breathing. If you are concerned with keeping time, there are so many apps on any of our digital products to sound an alarm when your allotted time is up. And if you want to engage in fancier meditation practices, there are also amazing apps and programs you can work with. I started with the Oprah Winfrey/Deepak Chopra free 21-day meditation challenge in 2013 and went from there.

> **#ElevateNOW: Just about anything can be a meditative practice if you set the intention to do so.**

If you want your walk in the park to be your meditation for the day, intend it to be so. If you take my friend Amy Jindra's advice, sex can be meditative. While you are immersed in your new meditative practices, don't allow fears of what may come up in meditation stop you from meditating. In all honesty, I don't always have earth-shattering, mind-blowing, life-changing revelations when I meditate. More often than not, I relax for a period of time and it feels good afterward. Other times, I am like, "Oh, well, I guess this is my new curriculum in my enlightenment". Just do it.

Your most basic tool in whatever you practice is having some sort of structure as well as regular practice. Regular practice allows for maintenance. You can keep it as basic as you want because if you don't give up the basics, you never have to go back to the basics. Ask people you know what practices have worked for them (and certainly feel free to reach out to me). I would also add to keep an open mind because what works for you today may not work for you later. Having an open mind will allow you to learn or intuitively be guided to another practice(s) that can work better for you today.

Beaming Down to Earth:

1. The person I wish to become—what do they look like? How do they see the world? How do they carry themselves in this world? How do they interact with others in this world?
2. What is some of the day-to-day stuff into which you could incorporate more intention? This could be as simple as riding the subway or going to the grocery store. Identify a few of these areas and start being more intentional.
3. Think of the spiritual practices you have heard of and were curious to try out. Now do one of each of those a day for the next couple of days.
4. What part of the day can you dedicate as little as five minutes to yourself to engage in a spiritual practice of your choosing? Start making this your enlightenment time on a daily basis.

Practicing your enlightenment in your daily life does not have to be super complicated. Remember that anything can be a spiritual practice if you intend it to be so. Be very clear as to what your intention is and it will help guide you to what your practices need to be. Don't be scared of using sex either, as some religions and dogmas will warn you against. If you keep your mind on the person you would like to become, all will fall into place.

My little gurus, we come to the end of our journey together here as we go into our final chapter, Oh My God, Buddha, Lady Gaga, and the Soul.

CHAPTER TWELVE

Oh My God, Buddha, Lady Gaga, and the Soul

"It doesn't matter if you love him, or capital H-I-M." - Lady Gaga

There are so many names for God. God, El, Jehovah, Shàngdi, Elohim, Allah, Hu, Parvardigar, and the list goes on and on. It's a wonder we don't know what to believe in except what our families tell us what to believe. When I was an adolescent, I came across a book on Greek gods and absolutely marveled at them. Apollo always seemed so cool to me, but so was Artemis. These were gods that were related as opposed to the God I was being taught in the Catholic Church. In comic books, I was introduced to Norse gods like Thor. This was really amazing because Thor hung out with The Avengers and some of the members were just humans and he was a god. Witches have male and female gods as well. Female gods seemed so cool to me, as I came from a very patriarchal upbringing. I learned about Lilith and immediately thought she was a badass. Yet there are so many gods that we really don't have a clear indication of which one is the one we should go to. It's like standing at a huge buffet and being overwhelmed with all the choices.

> **#ElevateNOW:** There is only one God/Source/
> Higher Power and it will show up for us the
> way we need to so we can understand it.

I have always felt that there is only one God/Higher Power/ Source. This entity is a combination of all the gods we know of throughout history. Before the Bible, the gods who were worshipped were traditionally female. This was what we could relate to at that time. God shows up in the form and fashion that we need it to show up in to understand it. This is presently the case for us today in our enlightenment.

> **#ElevateNOW: The most enlightened thing we can do is to believe in a God, or power greater than ourselves, who is loving and nonjudgmental.**

In my time with Twelve-Step programs, my favorite step I worked was the second. This step goes as follows: "We came to believe that a power greater than ourselves could restore us to sanity". My sponsor at the time asked me to write down the qualities of a Higher Power as this would be the Higher Power I would work with in subsequent steps. His only instruction was to make it "loving and forgiving". I cowered at the thought because I was sure that the Catholic God I was raised to believe would strike me down at the notion of creating another God. Fear stopped me moving forward as all of the Catholic guilt came flooding in. However, I was fortunate enough that I really respected my sponsor and trusted he knew what he was doing.

I didn't keep that journal, unfortunately, so I cannot list what I had written down back in 1999 when I did my second step. I will tell you that the last thing I wrote down was, 'He would be my superhero'. This statement caused all kinds of bells and whistles to go off. I can definitely relate to a superhero and in my years of reading comic books, I knew of a lot of superheroes. My Higher Power could very well be a Superman. Superman, and superheroes in general, were always a power greater than myself.

This clicked instantly for me and my ability to have intention in creating my own sense of enlightenment began. Superman, and superheroes in general, were beings to look up to in how they were portrayed. Even Superman had human struggles, despite not being human. The notion of superheroes was definitely a power greater than myself in my adolescence as my deep absorption into the fictional world allowed me to forget the feelings of suicide I struggled with. If they kept me alive then, they would definitely keep me sober. Did I pray to Superman? No, but I did try to see God at the time as a superhero instead of what He/She had been portrayed to me throughout my life. God as a super-hero was a concept I could work with.

Since creating this superhero God for myself two decades ago, my relationship with God has changed form. Today, my relationship with God is a continual process of getting in touch with my inner champion, the part of me most connected with the Universe, and embodying that into my daily life. While I still fail, and will continue to fail from time to time, I take stock of where I missed the mark and make a commitment to do better next time. My relationship with God today is recognizing that I am a part of God, much like a sunbeam is part of the sun. There is a main source of energy, but I am always connected to it. The times I forget my connection are the times I am not living my most enlightened self. I try to see God in everything. This one is the hardest to consistently succeed in as the world is filled with horrible people (some of whom I am related to or have been in relationships with). However, I main-tain the hope that I will see the God in them as much as I can see it in myself.

To the reader, I did use male pronouns for my Higher Power at the time only because this was all I knew. In my path, I have come to believe and recognize both the Divine Masculine and the Divine Feminine in my life. Also, I have come to believe that

I don't need a forgiving God because forgiving implies judgment. My God today is nonjudgmental, thus eliminating the need for forgiveness.

I initially had problems with the phrase, "power greater than ourselves"; the inner victimizer would take that and use it to its advantage by reminding me how inferior I am to God, and in life in general. This term is used purposely in Twelve-Step programs because substance abusers are typically considered to be control freaks and what keeps them in active addiction is their belief that they can control their addiction. To be able to have freedom from active addiction, part of their recovery involves them coming to believe that something other than themselves can do for them what they are unable to do alone. Therefore, "greater than" is less about inferiority or power and more about leaning on something other than yourself to help you be free of the chains that bind you.

This talk of creating our own God may seem very scary, but the reality is that what we were forced to believe in is just as scary. It almost tells us that our free will, our ability to discern and choose for ourselves, is not important. If listing the qualities of what you would want in your God, have a look at how you would want to feel in your personal relationship with God.

#ElevateNOW: In creating a personal relationship with God, focus on how you would want to feel in this relationship.

Knowing how you would want to feel is a very important aspect of our enlightenment. We discussed how this is vital in the Law of Attraction. So, it is here. The only problem with God is that we don't have a true physical presence as we would all of our other relationships; thus, focusing on the emotional aspect of the relationship is key. What have you always wanted to feel in your relationship with God/Higher Power/Source?

So much of this book is essentially deprogramming all the crap the inner victimizer has had us believe about ourselves our whole life. It likes to say we are sinners, we are not good enough, we will never be forgiven, we will always be judged negatively by others, who are you to create your own God, or any combination of these (and even more that I didn't list here). This is where intention once again comes into play.

> **#ElevateNOW: To be enlightened and have a relationship with a God of our understanding, we have to intend to be actively mindful of our own presence.**

There is this saying, "We are spiritual beings having a human existence." Whether you believe in this statement or not, being enlightened does not mean we will be free of bad things or negative events. Our belief in a God of our understanding will help us deal with these very real and human experiences better than the inner victimizer ever can.

If you are having trouble conceiving of a God of your understanding, I am going to give you an easy out. Make it the exact opposite of the inner victimizer and go from there. We know we don't want the inner victimizer in charge, so why not create one we do want in charge? This God can effectively manage the inner victimizer because it embodies love and nonjudgment. It can shrug off anything the inner victimizer can throw at you under any circumstances.

This thought of creating our own God will create fear of judgment from others. The beauty in having this relationship with a power greater than yourself is that you can keep it to yourself if you choose to. The key is to embed this relationship into your daily life instead of preaching about it like some of the di*ks we know.

Beaming Down to Earth:

1. If you could create your own God/Higher Power/Source, what would that look like for you?
2. How would you want to feel in your personal relationship with your God/Higher Power/Source?
3. How can you embody this for yourself in your daily life?
4. With the tools you have acquired in this book, how can you now create your best life?

So many of us have lived our lives in fear or confusion or disbelief of a God. In our path towards enlightenment, we don't have to feel any of this anymore. We have the power to create a power greater than ourselves, one of our own understanding. We can have the personal relationship with God we have always wanted. As long as you stick to something that is loving, nonjudgmental, and greater than you, you will be quite enlightened.

To the readers: Thank you for taking this journey with me. My sincerest wish is that you find enlightenment in anything and everything. I wish that you find the highest version of yourself on your own and live in that being as much as you can. I wish for you to feel empowered to live your best life. I wish for you to be able to handle life's adversities with more ease and less anger and hatred. My greatest wish, though, is that you will live a life Enlightened as Hell.

BONUS CHAPTER

How to Be Enlightened as
Hell – Drag Queen Style

Drag queen quotes have been inserted rather purposely at the start of every chapter. I did this for two reasons: I get annoyed at authors who want to impress you with some earth-shattering quote they found on the internet, and I am not that guy. Secondly, drag queens are the epitome of showing what's inside on the outside and doing it in as genuine and authentic way as they can. Drag queens are Enlightened as Hell because they don't give AF. It's part of what makes them successful. In this bonus chapter, I pull some of my favorite quotes from drag queens and provide interpretations of these quotes that will further make you Enlightened as Hell.

"Drag doesn't cover who you are; it reveals who you are." - RuPaul

Mama Ru. The drag superstar of the world. One of my favorite things about watching *RuPaul's Drag Race* is when he is in the workroom providing really enlightened suggestions to the contestants. What I particularly like about this quote is that it speaks to our inner champion. Drag is all about letting go of conformity. It allows you to express yourself in ways you may not ordinarily, or feel that you can't. While some may think drag queens are hiding behind makeup and clothing, I think they are showing us all the elements of themselves without the restrictions we or others impose upon us. In drag, they are free to be whoever they want to be. In your enlightenment, make sure to reveal who you are. If you need some makeup and a sequin dress, go for it. **Who you are is your enlightenment.**

"Your belief is a belief. My existence is a reality." - Divina DeCampo

This one hit me like a ton of bricks during the first season of *RuPaul's Drag Race UK*. Divina was chatting with her fellow queens about marriage equality and how many people are still not with the notion. Her epic retort is a priceless gem in our quest for enlightenment. Generally speaking, never let anyone tell you what is right or wrong for you. That is their belief and it does not have to be your reality. This goes for your inner victimizer. You can even tell your inner victimizer that, because it's the inner victimizer's beliefs and not yours. Sure, the inner victimizer is a part of you, but it is not you. Therefore, its beliefs are not your reality. **Your reality is your enlightenment.**

"When do I get to blow them? I can't say that? I can't say that either?" - Katya

Katya has always been my spirit animal. She was so verbal about her insecurities and anxieties. When twenty men in Speedos and oiled-up skin showed up in the workroom for a mini challenge, this was Katya's first thought, and I am here for that. This was her truth at that very moment and part of our path towards enlightenment is to speak our truth. While there are times we must use prudence and discretion, most times we need to just speak our truths and not judge ourselves for our truths. At that moment, Katya's first urge was to perform mass fellatio. Trust me, she was not the only one thinking that. **Owning your truth is your enlightenment.**

"For all the queens telling me that I am not polished enough: I just want them to know that I'm polish remover, b*tch." - Adore Delano

It's no secret to anyone who knows me well that Adore is one of my favorite drag queens and in my fantasy world, she is my drag mom. What I have always admired about her is that she owned herself in a way that most queens don't in the face of being in a competition with more "polished" queens. She was okay with not being at the level of someone of Bianca Del Rio's stature and fought her way to the top three of her season, along with Bianca herself. You don't have to be like someone else to be a winner. You get to define who you are. If you worry that you are not as good as someone else, you won't be a winner. You have what it takes to be a winner, baby, so be a winner regardless of anything. **Defining who you are is your enlightenment.**

"I'm ready for another week of me doing mediocre." - Cheryl Hole

Cheryl Hole is one of my other favorite drag queens. I had the absolute pleasure of having her host my launch event in London for my second book. I knew she was the right queen to host the event as she went on to be in the top four without ever having won a main challenge. Regardless of this, she put forth everything she had despite her lack of wins. One week, after a particularly grueling set of critiques, Cheryl walked into the workroom and said this statement. There are times in life when mediocre is okay, as long as we don't stay there. We need always to strive to be our very best, but we don't always have to be the best. If we really take ourselves out of the equation, what we deem as mediocre is really just the inner victimizer acting up again. Did you do your best and you know you did in your heart? That's all that matters (though maybe not always on a competition show). **Knowing who you are despite critiques is your enlightenment.**

"I feel sexy in anything, even a body bag." - Sharon Needles

We get to talk about sex again. While not one of my particular favorites, Sharon Needles was the first drag queen on the show that really pushed the limits of drag. Many referred to her as "the spooky queen." Despite criticisms from her peers, she went on to win her season of "Drag Race." What she is saying here is all about being comfortable in your own skin. If she can feel sexy in a body bag, you can feel sexy no matter what. We can get so caught up on how we look on the outside that the insides turn into mush. We look great on the outside, but inside, we are d*cks. Who you are is sexy and that is what will turn someone else on. **Knowing how sexy you are is your enlightenment.**

"If I wanted to come for you I'd come into your room at night and cut your wigs up." - Bianca Del Rio

Ah, Bianca and her Rolodex of hate. She definitely kept her fellow contestants on their toes during her season. She is by far the most recognized drag queen, after RuPaul herself. One of the things I admired greatly about Bianca is that everyone always knew where they stood with her. So many times, especially when interacting with others on social media, we don't know who we are dealing with. Other times, we are not our authentic selves. However, if we take a cue from Bianca, it would be in our best interest of our enlightenment to be as authentic as possible so people know whose presence they are in. **Being our authentic selves so people know where they stand with us is your enlightenment.**

"I kind of have this mentality that says, everything works out in the end. And if it's not working out, it's not the end." - Bob the Drag Queen

Bob the Drag Queen, as opposed to Bob the Spiritual Guru, is probably my favorite winner on "Drag Race." I really feel she killed her season and, despite the judge's critiques, also won her season. Her statement feels like it was her attitude the entire season. She never gave up. She didn't see negative critiques or being in the bottom as the end for her. She knew what worked for her was being the winner and that was what she strived for, even when she was lip-syncing for her life. She continually chose to see things differently. She saw what her outcome was going to be and went for it. How you see things makes all the difference along your spiritual path. **The ability to see things differently is your enlightenment.**

"There's always time for a cocktail." - Mrs. Kasha Davis

Mrs. Kasha Davis is such a talented queen and unfortunately, we did not get to see her full range in her season on "Drag Race." However, her signature line stuck in everyone's head because it was so catchy and when applied to our spiritual journey, so poignant. Our primary goal in life is to take care of ourselves. When we think we don't have time, we need to remember "there's always time for a cocktail." You may substitute anything for a cocktail and still make it self-care. Take time for yourself to do something good for you. We talked about how taking just three minutes a day for meditation can do wonders. Let's tack another three minutes for some other self-care activity. If it's a cocktail, great. **Self-care is your enlightenment.**

"I feel very attacked right now!" - Laganja Estranga

This is by far the most popular meme amongst my friends, Laganja Estranga telling her peers that she's feeling attacked. When it seems that the world is ganging up on us, we can certainly feel attacked, but we don't have to stay in this mentality. At some point, we need to be our own victor and do something to change our perception of things. We need to choose to see something differently. We could also do well to forgive. **Forgiveness is your enlightenment.**

"Check your lipstick before you come for me." - Naomi Smalls

Remember that saying, "check yourself before you wreck yourself"? If we choose to come for someone, let's be very clear where we ourselves are at. Also, when someone attacks you, it means more about them than it does about you. Knowing this difference is so essential in our spiritual journey because we will be met with opposition and adversity. **Knowing yourself and others is your enlightenment.**

"I don't get cute. I get drop-dead gorgeous." - Alyssa Edwards

I simply love me some Alyssa Edwards. She is just a phenomenal queen. Seeing her development over the various seasons of *Drag Race* is so inspiring. She was cute but she didn't stay cute. She did get drop-dead gorgeous. She reminds me of the quote from *The Velvet Rage*, "What would the person I wish to become do in this situation?" Alyssa had a sh*t ton of adversity and she is a very popular queen. When faced with adversity, she likely asked herself, "Who do I want to be?" The answer was "drop-dead gorgeous." **Going towards the person you wish to be is your enlightenment.**

At the end of the day, to be a success in *RuPaul's Drag Race*, you must embody Charisma, Uniqueness, Nerve, and Talent. These are definitely qualities that would benefit all of us on our path to enlightenment. So instead of being a d*ck, be a C . . . U . . . N . . . T! Namaste.

BV - #0103 - 250822 - C0 - 198/129/7 - PB - 9781399930161 - Matt Lamination